# JUMBLE®

# Vacation

**Take a Break from Boredom with These Puzzles!**

Jeff Knurek,
Mike Argirion,
and
David L. Hoyt

# TRIUMPH
## B O O K S

This book is available in quantity at special discounts
for your group or organization.

For further information, contact:

Triumph Books LLC
814 North Franklin Street
Chicago, Illinois 60610
Phone: (312) 337-0747
www.triumphbooks.com


Printed in U.S.A.

ISBN: 978-1-60078-796-6


Design by Sue Knopf

# CONTENTS

# JUMBLE®

# Vacation

## Classic Puzzles

# JUMBLE®

Unscramble these four Jumbles, one letter to
each square, to form four ordinary words.

KLAYN

PEBID

ENCOUP

LEWBIA

What's
that
noise?

It's
4 A.M.

WHAT THE SLEEP-
ING RECRUITS FELT
LIKE WHEN THEY
HEARD THE BUGLE.

Now arrange the circled letters to form
the surprise answer, as suggested by the
above cartoon.

*Print answer here* ◯◯◯◯◯ " ◯◯ "

# JUMBLE®

Unscramble these four Jumbles, one letter to each square, to form four ordinary words.

MERFA

GAMLE

YIVELT

OPTECK

How romantic

It seems like you could reach out and touch it

WHEN THEY VIEWED THE FULL MOON FROM THE MOUN-TAIN TOP, THEY COULDN'T---

Now arrange the circled letters to form the surprise answer, as suggested by the above cartoon.

**Print answer here** ⬡⬡⬡ ⬡⬡⬡⬡ IT

3

# JUMBLE®

Unscramble these four Jumbles, one letter to each square, to form four ordinary words.

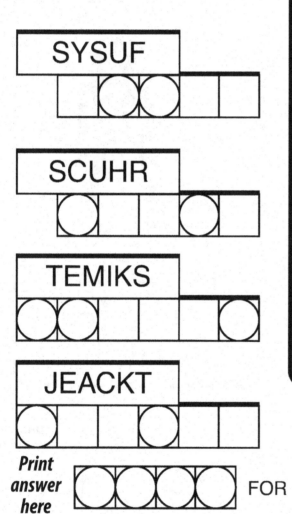

SYSUF

SCUHR

TEMIKS

JEACKT

Maybe it will improve my footwork

WHY THE BOXER JOINED THE SOCCER TEAM.

Now arrange the circled letters to form the surprise answer, as suggested by the above cartoon.

*Print answer here*

FOR "            "

4

# JUMBLE®

Unscramble these four Jumbles, one letter to each square, to form four ordinary words.

LOBAT

GALEE

THEVIR

NUCKOL

WHEN THE DENTIST AND HIS MANICURIST WIFE FOUGHT, IT WAS———

Now arrange the circled letters to form the surprise answer, as suggested by the above cartoon.

**Print answer here** ◯◯◯◯◯ AND ◯◯◯◯

# JUMBLE®

Unscramble these four Jumbles, one letter to
each square, to form four ordinary words.

AKDEB

RUPUS

DECLUD

CADDIN

He's been
raised well

WHERE IDEALS
CAN COME FROM.

Now arrange the circled letters to form
the surprise answer, as suggested by the
above cartoon.

*Print answer here*

# JUMBLE®

Unscramble these four Jumbles, one letter to each square, to form four ordinary words.

HICCK

TOAQU

MAZECE

COMEEB

I'll do better next time

WHAT THE BOOMERANG CHAMPION SOUGHT WHEN HE LOST THE CONTEST.

Now arrange the circled letters to form the surprise answer, as suggested by the above cartoon.

*Print answer here* A " ◯◯◯◯◯◯◯◯ "

7

# JUMBLE®

Unscramble these four Jumbles, one letter to each square, to form four ordinary words.

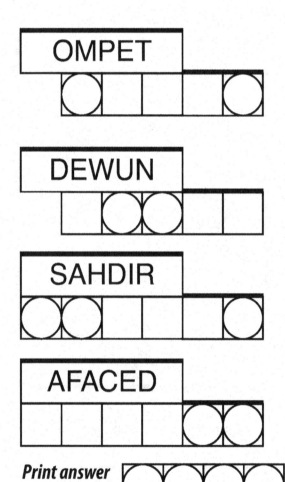

OMPET

DEWUN

SAHDIR

AFACED

He treats us as equals

Doesn't put on any airs

THE STUDENTS ADMIRED THE ARCHAEOLOGIST BECAUSE HE WAS----

Now arrange the circled letters to form the surprise answer, as suggested by the above cartoon.

*Print answer here*  ⬡⬡⬡⬡ TO ⬡⬡⬡⬡⬡

# JUMBLE®

Unscramble these four Jumbles, one letter to each square, to form four ordinary words.

GUBOS

FLECT

MIULEH

CHYSIP

Berg straight ahead!

WHAT IT TAKES TO SPOT A DISTANT ICE SITE.

Now arrange the circled letters to form the surprise answer, as suggested by the above cartoon.

*Print answer here*

# JUMBLE®

Unscramble these four Jumbles, one letter to
each square, to form four ordinary words.

YERAW

POCHE

FITTOU

FARREY

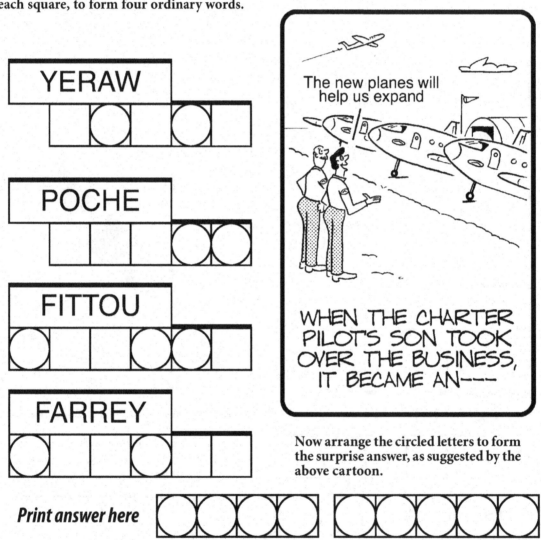

The new planes will help us expand

WHEN THE CHARTER
PILOT'S SON TOOK
OVER THE BUSINESS,
IT BECAME AN----

Now arrange the circled letters to form
the surprise answer, as suggested by the
above cartoon.

**Print answer here** ⬭⬭⬭⬭ ⬭⬭⬭⬭⬭

# JUMBLE®

Unscramble these four Jumbles, one letter to each square, to form four ordinary words.

GEFUD

MYKUR

NIWWON

REYJES

I'm so happy. Can I have the keys, Mom?

THE FIRST THING THE TEEN TOOK WHEN HE GOT HIS DRIVER'S LICENSE.

Now arrange the circled letters to form the surprise answer, as suggested by the above cartoon.

*Print answer here* A " ☐☐☐ " ☐☐☐☐

# JUMBLE®

Unscramble these four Jumbles, one letter to
each square, to form four ordinary words.

PYPIN

SELOO

DOBENY

CAFEED

Nothing special
these days

Your sandwich, sir

WHAT AIR TRAVEL-
ERS GET, EVEN IN
FIRST CLASS.

Now arrange the circled letters to form
the surprise answer, as suggested by the
above cartoon.

Print answer
here
"⬡⬡⬡⬡⬡" ⬡⬡⬡⬡

# JUMBLE®

Unscramble these four Jumbles, one letter to each square, to form four ordinary words.

TULIB

TARAL

HERNUT

DORVOE

Now we won't have to drag everything

WHEN THE WHEEL WAS INVENTED, IT CREATED A---

Now arrange the circled letters to form the surprise answer, as suggested by the above cartoon.

Print answer here

# JUMBLE®

Unscramble these four Jumbles, one letter to each square, to form four ordinary words.

TYJET

MESOU

LOMBAG

SUTHPY

Let's have another round

IN A BAR, SITTING DOWN CAN RESULT IN---

Now arrange the circled letters to form the surprise answer, as suggested by the above cartoon.

*Print answer here*

# JUMBLE®

Unscramble these four Jumbles, one letter to
each square, to form four ordinary words.

DIMIO

TAUID

GYSSAR

THERTE

It's supposed
to go into
the pail

WHEN THE CITY
SLICKER TRIED
MILKING A COW,
THE RESULT WAS----

Now arrange the circled letters to form
the surprise answer, as suggested by the
above cartoon.

Print
answer AN "⬡⬡⬡⬡⬡" ⬡⬡⬡⬡
here

# JUMBLE®

Unscramble these four Jumbles, one letter to
each square, to form four ordinary words.

ELLIB

KIRPE

NUCLUR

ELDAHN

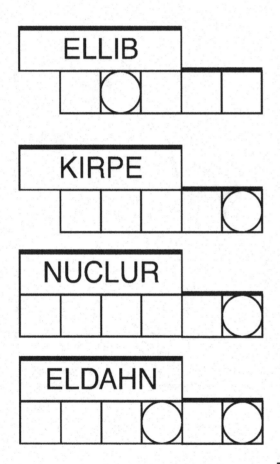

You're fired, you lazy...

ONE RESULT OF
BEING RILED.

Now arrange the circled letters to form
the surprise answer, as suggested by the
above cartoon.

*Print answer here*

# JUMBLE®

Unscramble these four Jumbles, one letter to
each square, to form four ordinary words.

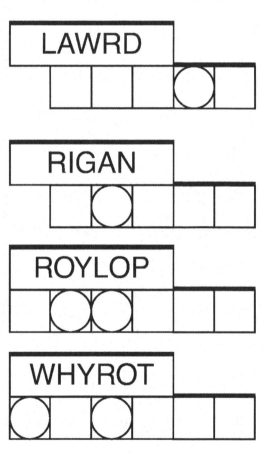

LAWRD

RIGAN

ROYLOP

WHYROT

Hey, those
are my seats!

Sez who?

A TICKETS MIX-UP
CAN RESULT IN A----

Now arrange the circled letters to form
the surprise answer, as suggested by the
above cartoon.

**Print answer here**

# JUMBLE®

Unscramble these four Jumbles, one letter to
each square, to form four ordinary words.

JAHAR

EBBIR

CAFFEE

GOINID

Time for dinner

No time.
Too much work

A BUSY
BLACKSMITH
WILL DO THIS.

Now arrange the circled letters to form
the surprise answer, as suggested by the
above cartoon.

Print
answer
here

"⬡⬡⬡⬡⬡" ⬡⬡⬡⬡⬡⬡

# JUMBLE®

Unscramble these four Jumbles, one letter to
each square, to form four ordinary words.

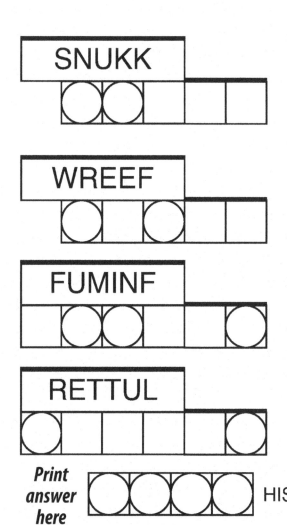

SNUKK

WREEF

FUMINF

RETTUL

HE WAS NAMED
TAXIDERMIST OF
THE YEAR BECAUSE
HE----

Now arrange the circled letters to form
the surprise answer, as suggested by the
above cartoon.

**Print answer here** ☐☐☐☐ HIS " ☐☐☐☐☐ "

# JUMBLE®

Unscramble these four Jumbles, one letter to each square, to form four ordinary words.

TIFEN

TIMAY

DRAWZI

MILSES

My chest is moving south

A MIDDLE-AGE PAUNCH CAN BE A----

Now arrange the circled letters to form the surprise answer, as suggested by the above cartoon.

Print answer here

" ☐☐☐☐☐ " OF ☐☐☐☐

# JUMBLE®

Unscramble these four Jumbles, one letter to each square, to form four ordinary words.

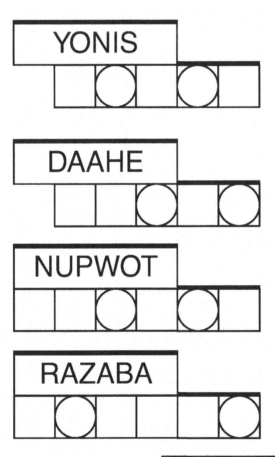

YONIS

DAAHE

NUPWOT

RAZABA

Try the meatball recipe. It's my favorite

BOOK SIGNING TODAY!

WHAT A COOKBOOK AUTHOR WILL DO.

Now arrange the circled letters to form the surprise answer, as suggested by the above cartoon.

**Print answer here** ⬡⬡⬡ HIS ⬡⬡⬡⬡⬡

# JUMBLE

Unscramble these four Jumbles, one letter to each square, to form four ordinary words.

NOPEY

MEFAD

DRIBLE

LAISEY

I'm busy with practice and homework

WHY THE YOUNG BALL PLAYER DIDN'T HAVE A STEADY GIRLFRIEND.

Now arrange the circled letters to form the surprise answer, as suggested by the above cartoon.

Print answer here

HE ◯◯◯◯◯◯ THE " ◯◯◯◯◯ "

# JUMBLE®

Unscramble these four Jumbles, one letter to
each square, to form four ordinary words.

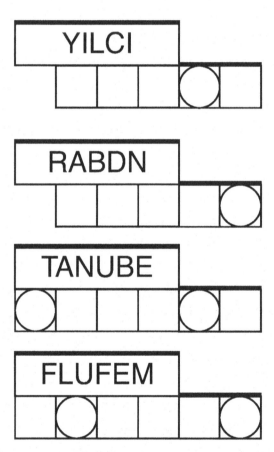

YILCI

RABDN

TANUBE

FLUFEM

Fill out the forms.
It will cost around
$50

WHAT IT TAKES TO
SHIP A PACKAGE
CROSS COUNTRY.

Now arrange the circled letters to form
the surprise answer, as suggested by the
above cartoon.

***Print answer here*** A "  "

# JUMBLE®

Unscramble these four Jumbles, one letter to each square, to form four ordinary words.

CEDDI

GIHLT

LAIFAC

TIGBLE

Happy Birthday!

Oh, boy. It's a kind of computer

GIVING JUNIOR A HEAP OF EDUCATIONAL TOYS MADE HIM A---

Now arrange the circled letters to form the surprise answer, as suggested by the above cartoon.

Print answer here

"☐☐☐☐☐☐" ☐☐☐☐☐

# JUMBLE®

Unscramble these four Jumbles, one letter to each square, to form four ordinary words.

ZAMIE

NAHCT

TARDIO

INTIEF

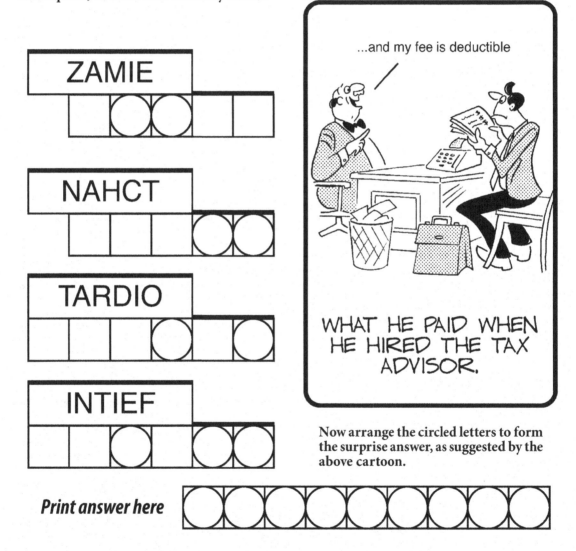

...and my fee is deductible

WHAT HE PAID WHEN HE HIRED THE TAX ADVISOR.

Now arrange the circled letters to form the surprise answer, as suggested by the above cartoon.

*Print answer here*

25

# JUMBLE®

Unscramble these four Jumbles, one letter to each square, to form four ordinary words.

BASAH

MARAD

STINCH

BROSAB

It's almost five o' clock

blah blah blah

THE SECRETARY CONCENTRATED ON THIS.

Now arrange the circled letters to form the surprise answer, as suggested by the above cartoon.

Print answer here   THE ⭕⭕⭕⭕⭕ ⭕⭕⭕⭕

# JUMBLE®

# Vacation

## Daily
## Puzzles

# JUMBLE®

Unscramble these four Jumbles, one letter to each square, to form four ordinary words.

UNOMT

SNAIE

MOSHNA

DEGUMS

Perfect.
Worth every penny

WHAT THE MALE
MODEL RECEIVED
WHEN HE POSED
IN THE SUIT.

Now arrange the circled letters to form the surprise answer, as suggested by the above cartoon.

Print
answer  A  "◯◯◯◯◯◯◯◯"  ◯◯◯
here

# JUMBLE®

Unscramble these four Jumbles, one letter to each square, to form four ordinary words.

VALIT

YOVIR

BINLEB

ANGOLS

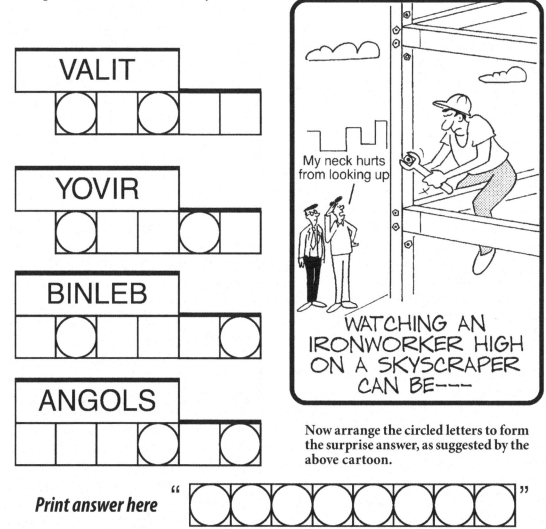

My neck hurts from looking up

WATCHING AN IRONWORKER HIGH ON A SKYSCRAPER CAN BE---

Now arrange the circled letters to form the surprise answer, as suggested by the above cartoon.

Print answer here " ◯◯◯◯◯◯◯◯◯ "

# JUMBLE®

Unscramble these four Jumbles, one letter to each square, to form four ordinary words.

LURBY

YLDMO

PORRAL

DRAFIT

He's a real daredevil

WHAT HE TURNED INTO WHEN HE WENT TO SKYDIVING SCHOOL.

Now arrange the circled letters to form the surprise answer, as suggested by the above cartoon.

**Print answer here** A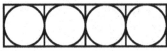

# JUMBLE®

Unscramble these four Jumbles, one letter to
each square, to form four ordinary words.

DEUXE

TILMI

GACHER

YAUNES

Whew, that was
a tough one

WHEN THE MECHANIC
INSTALLED THE
NEW MUFFLER, IT
WAS----

Now arrange the circled letters to form
the surprise answer, as suggested by the
above cartoon.

Print
answer
here

" "

# JUMBLE®

Unscramble these four Jumbles, one letter to each square, to form four ordinary words.

BUTIC

NARCK

GURCOH

GOAFER

I always wanted a convertible and I got a good deal

WHAT HE DROVE WHEN HE BOUGHT A USED CAR.

Now arrange the circled letters to form the surprise answer, as suggested by the above cartoon.

Print answer here  A

# JUMBLE®

Unscramble these four Jumbles, one letter to each square, to form four ordinary words.

OGOIL

NEKEL

WURPAD

KLYFNU

WHEN SHE CHANGED HER HAIR COLOR, IT WAS———

Now arrange the circled letters to form the surprise answer, as suggested by the above cartoon.

*Print answer here*  TO "◯◯◯" ◯◯◯

# JUMBLE®

Unscramble these four Jumbles, one letter to
each square, to form four ordinary words.

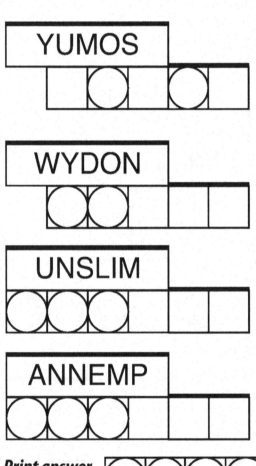

YUMOS

WYDON

UNSLIM

ANNEMP

It'll cost you a pretty
pence but I get results

TRAINER

WHAT IT COST THE
LONDON MOGUL
TO LOSE SOME
POUNDS.

Now arrange the circled letters to form
the surprise answer, as suggested by the
above cartoon.

*Print answer
here*

# JUMBLE®

Unscramble these four Jumbles, one letter to each square, to form four ordinary words.

**RYTUL**

**OSSUE**

**ENMUIM**

**THELAH**

Your eggs, gentlemen

Let's look over this report

WHAT THE BUSINESSMEN READ BEFORE BREAKFAST.

Now arrange the circled letters to form the surprise answer, as suggested by the above cartoon.

*Print answer here* 

# JUMBLE®

Unscramble these four Jumbles, one letter to each square, to form four ordinary words.

TCHAB

NOPER

RUBECH

SMALEY

Let's lie in the sun until our hair dries

WHAT THE TEEN-AGERS TURNED INTO AFTER A DIP IN THE OCEAN.

Now arrange the circled letters to form the surprise answer, as suggested by the above cartoon.

Print answer here

# JUMBLE®

Unscramble these four Jumbles, one letter to each square, to form four ordinary words.

ENDUC

ZENOO

REZIFE

HUBILS

The one and only...

WHEN THE CATS PERFORMED FOR THE ANIMAL TRAINER, HE WAS----

Now arrange the circled letters to form the surprise answer, as suggested by the above cartoon.

**Print answer here** " ◯◯◯◯◯◯◯◯ "

# JUMBLE®

Unscramble these four Jumbles, one letter to each square, to form four ordinary words.

GUVEA

DYPET

UNRICH

VARMEL

Look at him go

WHAT THE SURGEON TURNED INTO AT THE ANNUAL PARTY.

Now arrange the circled letters to form the surprise answer, as suggested by the above cartoon.

**Print answer here**  A

# JUMBLE®

Unscramble these four Jumbles, one letter to
each square, to form four ordinary words.

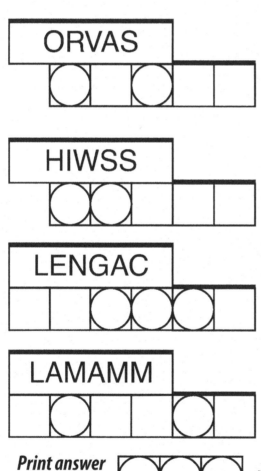

ORVAS

HIWSS

LENGAC

LAMAMM

**Print answer here**

A

It is the very fiber of my work

WHEN THE ARTIST
WAS ASKED WHAT
WAS BEHIND THE
PAINTING, HE SAID
IT---

Now arrange the circled letters to form
the surprise answer, as suggested by the
above cartoon.

# JUMBLE®

Unscramble these four Jumbles, one letter to
each square, to form four ordinary words.

IMCUS

FAHFC

CHOROT

HAMMEY

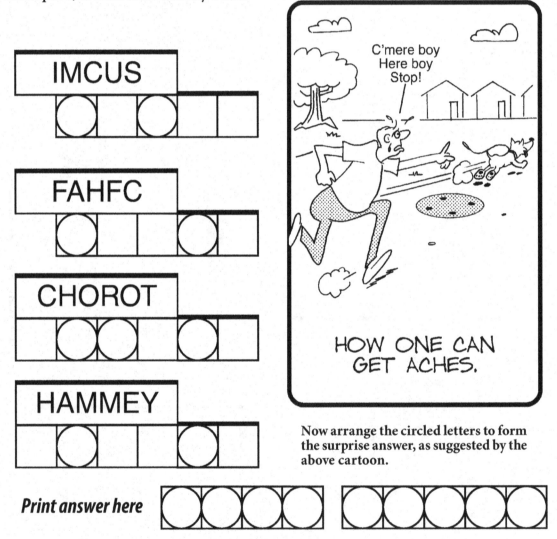

HOW ONE CAN
GET ACHES.

Now arrange the circled letters to form
the surprise answer, as suggested by the
above cartoon.

**Print answer here**

# JUMBLE®

Unscramble these four Jumbles, one letter to each square, to form four ordinary words.

CNOTH

TAULD

TOGIER

SOYRAV

Watch me. Then keep practicing

WHEN THE BALLET STAR HELPED HER DANCEMATE, SHE DID A----

Now arrange the circled letters to form the surprise answer, as suggested by the above cartoon.

**Print answer here** ⬡⬡⬡⬡ " ⬡⬡⬡⬡ "

# JUMBLE®

Unscramble these four Jumbles, one letter to
each square, to form four ordinary words.

FALEY

HINKT

HERITH

SPRAYT

$10,000!
That's twice the estimate.
I'm not paying

WHAT HAPPENED
WHEN HE GOT THE
BILL FOR THE
ROOF?

Now arrange the circled letters to form
the surprise answer, as suggested by the
above cartoon.

*Print
answer
here*  HE ⬡⬡⬡ THE " ⬡⬡⬡⬡⬡⬡⬡ "

# JUMBLE®

Unscramble these four Jumbles, one letter to each square, to form four ordinary words.

VARGE

BOSEE

BABRYC

SMIBUT

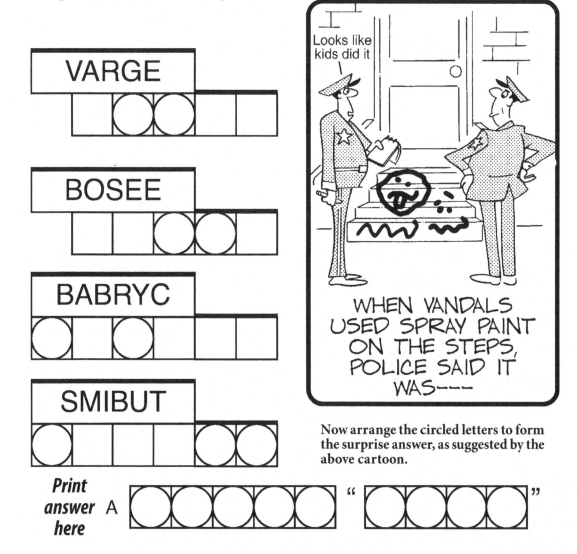

Looks like kids did it

WHEN VANDALS USED SPRAY PAINT ON THE STEPS, POLICE SAID IT WAS ⎯ ⎯ ⎯

Now arrange the circled letters to form the surprise answer, as suggested by the above cartoon.

**Print answer here** A ⬡⬡⬡⬡⬡ " ⬡⬡⬡⬡ "

# JUMBLE®

Unscramble these four Jumbles, one letter to each square, to form four ordinary words.

RIMEN

BYGAG

TRAUGI

DEPHUL

More wattage and less cost

WHAT THE COUPLE GOT IN THE LIGHTING STORE.

Now arrange the circled letters to form the surprise answer, as suggested by the above cartoon.

Print answer here    A " ⬡⬡⬡⬡⬡⬡ "   ⬡⬡⬡⬡

# JUMBLE®

Unscramble these four Jumbles, one letter to
each square, to form four ordinary words.

LIWLT

CHARP

DEECES

TEAZOL

Not my style

WHY THE YOUNG
KING REFUSED TO
WEAR A CROWN.

Now arrange the circled letters to form
the surprise answer, as suggested by the
above cartoon.

Print
answer
here

IT ⬡⬡⬡ ⬡⬡⬡ " ⬡⬡⬡ "

# JUMBLE®

Unscramble these four Jumbles, one letter to each square, to form four ordinary words.

CIMEN

LASIA

BLIMEN

SYTHAN

No raises. Let's step it up

The less he pays us the more he makes

THE WORKERS DESCRIBED THE NASTY TYCOON AS---

Now arrange the circled letters to form the surprise answer, as suggested by the above cartoon.

Print answer here  A ◯◯◯ OF " ◯◯◯◯◯ "

# JUMBLE®

Unscramble these four Jumbles, one letter to
each square, to form four ordinary words.

BADIE

DONSY

BADCUT

GRUNNE

This isn't my favorite chore

WHEN MOM SEWED
THE HOLE IN HIS
SOCK, SHE CON-
SIDERED IT A---

Now arrange the circled letters to form
the surprise answer, as suggested by the
above cartoon.

Print
answer
here

" "

# JUMBLE®

Unscramble these four Jumbles, one letter to
each square, to form four ordinary words.

SNAIB

SCEHS

LIMNAR

TUSHIA

Danny Dreamboat just
slammed into Harry Handsome

ONE MIGHT SAY
THAT THE MOVIE
STARS TURNED
THE DEMOLITION
DERBY INTO A----

Now arrange the circled letters to form
the surprise answer, as suggested by the
above cartoon.

*Print answer here* " ⬡⬡⬡⬡⬡ " ⬡⬡⬡

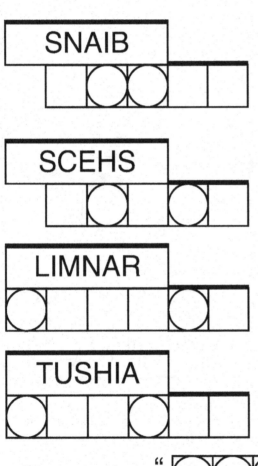

# JUMBLE®

Unscramble these four Jumbles, one letter to each square, to form four ordinary words.

KAYWG

KULCC

HARTTO

NURTAT

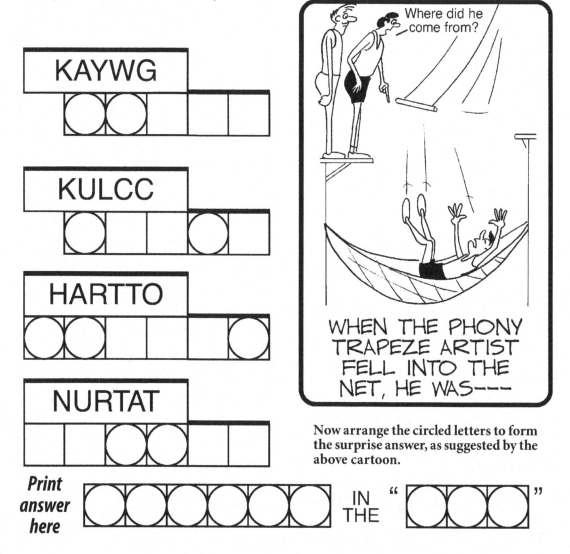

Where did he come from?

WHEN THE PHONY TRAPEZE ARTIST FELL INTO THE NET, HE WAS----

Now arrange the circled letters to form the surprise answer, as suggested by the above cartoon.

Print answer here

IN THE " "

# JUMBLE®

Unscramble these four Jumbles, one letter to
each square, to form four ordinary words.

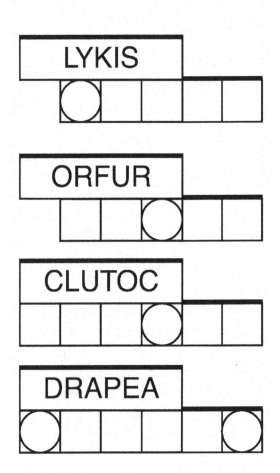

LYKIS

ORFUR

CLUTOC

DRAPEA

The winner gets the big money

WHAT A BOXER
WILL FIGHT FOR
THAT A WOMAN HAS.

Now arrange the circled letters to form
the surprise answer, as suggested by the
above cartoon.

*Print answer here* A ⬡⬡⬡⬡⬡

# JUMBLE

Unscramble these four Jumbles, one letter to
each square, to form four ordinary words.

GLUHC

CAPIN

RECUPS

SCIBEP

Home of the one-minute haircut

WHEN THE CREW
LINED UP FOR
HAIRCUTS, THE
SUBMARINE
BECAME---

Now arrange the circled letters to form
the surprise answer, as suggested by the
above cartoon.

Print
answer   A "⬡⬡⬡⬡⬡⬡⬡" ⬡⬡⬡⬡
here

# JUMBLE

Unscramble these four Jumbles, one letter to
each square, to form four ordinary words.

POCUE

DREEL

AXNYRL

EXDULE

Drinks are on me

He wins
again

WHAT THE JANITOR
DID WHEN HE
PLAYED POKER.

Now arrange the circled letters to form
the surprise answer, as suggested by the
above cartoon.

Print
answer
here

HE " ⃝⃝⃝⃝⃝⃝⃝ " ⃝⃝

# JUMBLE®

Unscramble these four Jumbles, one letter to each square, to form four ordinary words.

CUPAN

ROLYG

SILCHE

LOTTEB

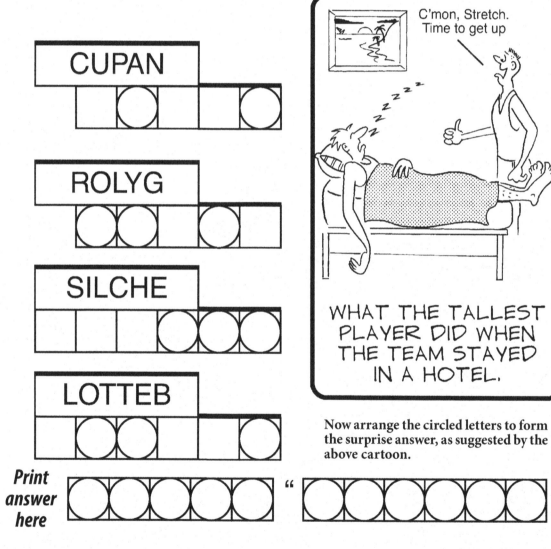

C'mon, Stretch.
Time to get up

WHAT THE TALLEST
PLAYER DID WHEN
THE TEAM STAYED
IN A HOTEL.

Now arrange the circled letters to form the surprise answer, as suggested by the above cartoon.

**Print answer here**  ⬡⬡⬡⬡⬡ " ⬡⬡⬡⬡⬡⬡ "

# JUMBLE®

Unscramble these four Jumbles, one letter to
each square, to form four ordinary words.

GLEEY

CADEY

HARPON

COATEL

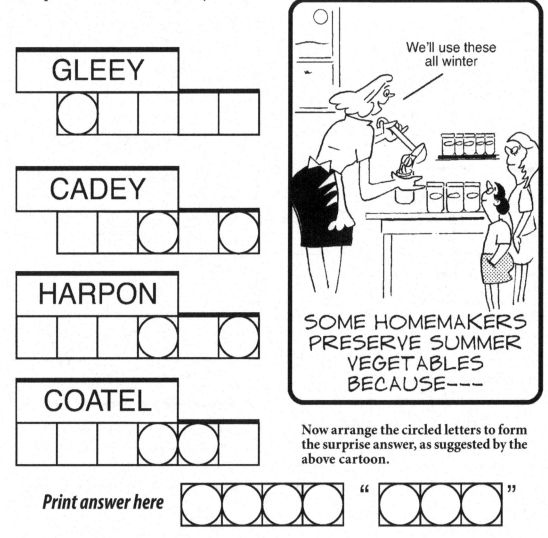

We'll use these
all winter

SOME HOMEMAKERS
PRESERVE SUMMER
VEGETABLES
BECAUSE---

Now arrange the circled letters to form
the surprise answer, as suggested by the
above cartoon.

**Print answer here** ◯◯◯◯ " ◯◯◯ "

# JUMBLE®

Unscramble these four Jumbles, one letter to each square, to form four ordinary words.

RUHTT

ILPAT

FOUNSI

LISGRY

Sorry, sir.
Can't find it

*!!@?*
Of all the
incompetent...

WHAT HAPPENED
WHEN HIS GRIP
WAS LOST.

Now arrange the circled letters to form the surprise answer, as suggested by the above cartoon.

Print
answer    HE ⬡⬡⬡⬡  ⬡⬡⬡  "⬡⬡⬡⬡"
here

# JUMBLE®

Unscramble these four Jumbles, one letter to
each square, to form four ordinary words.

ILVIC

RECEL

TAEGOE

PACALA

You must've
liked the food

WHEN THE SKINNY
LITTLE CONVICT
GAINED WEIGHT IN
PRISON, HE WAS----

Now arrange the circled letters to form
the surprise answer, as suggested by the
above cartoon.

*Print answer here* " "

# JUMBLE®

Unscramble these four Jumbles, one letter to each square, to form four ordinary words.

YONIR

WHEGI

HYWINN

NAUSED

Go buy yourself something

That's a $2,000 pot

SHE WAS ATTRACTED TO THE CARD SHARK BECAUSE HE HAD----

Now arrange the circled letters to form the surprise answer, as suggested by the above cartoon.

Print answer here " ⬡⬡⬡⬡⬡⬡⬡ " ⬡⬡⬡⬡

# JUMBLE®

Unscramble these four Jumbles, one letter to
each square, to form four ordinary words.

KREPY

HELAT

DRALIA

SPELTE

IN THE OLD WEST,
A SIX-SHOOTER
WAS AN ----

Now arrange the circled letters to form
the surprise answer, as suggested by the
above cartoon.

Print
answer
here
"          "

# JUMBLE®

Unscramble these four Jumbles, one letter to each square, to form four ordinary words.

VEALE

PODEK

FISHTE

RAMTRY

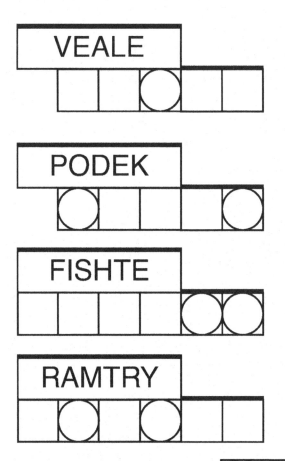

I'll never get married again

Goodbye!

SHE DUMPED HER BOYFRIEND BE-CAUSE SHE WANTED A FUTURE AND HE----

Now arrange the circled letters to form the surprise answer, as suggested by the above cartoon.

**Print answer here** ⬡⬡⬡ A ⬡⬡⬡⬡

# JUMBLE®

Unscramble these four Jumbles, one letter to each square, to form four ordinary words.

AMELY

BIBAR

LOUBED

RICHEP

Get the dogs and set up roadblocks

WHAT THE WARDEN DID WHEN THE CROOKED BARBER ESCAPED.

Now arrange the circled letters to form the surprise answer, as suggested by the above cartoon.

Print answer here "⃝⃝⃝⃝⃝⃝" THE ⃝⃝⃝⃝

# JUMBLE®

Unscramble these four Jumbles, one letter to each square, to form four ordinary words.

ROPIR

SIFIN

FITANN

MELING

They used to cost a quarter

$2.00

WHY THE BALLOONS WENT UP.

Now arrange the circled letters to form the surprise answer, as suggested by the above cartoon.

Print answer here "⬡⬡⬡⬡⬡⬡⬡⬡⬡"

# JUMBLE®

Unscramble these four Jumbles, one letter to each square, to form four ordinary words.

UNGED

ELBIG

RIDOLF

REDDEG

He's always hoeing or weeding

WHAT THE VIOLINIST ENJOYED DOING IN THE GARDEN.

Now arrange the circled letters to form the surprise answer, as suggested by the above cartoon.

Print answer here " ◯◯◯◯◯◯◯◯ "

# JUMBLE®

Unscramble these four Jumbles, one letter to each square, to form four ordinary words.

ILLSE

DIMAT

CHETOL

THINGK

Another round on me

Jim always buys

BEING LOOSE WITH MONEY CAN LEAD TO THIS.

Now arrange the circled letters to form the surprise answer, as suggested by the above cartoon.

Print answer here "◯◯◯◯◯" ◯◯◯◯◯

# JUMBLE®

Unscramble these four Jumbles, one letter to
each square, to form four ordinary words.

KLANF

YEJON

TOOMIN

LAFTER

Do you know
who I am?

Your seat, sir

WHEN THE
CELEBRITY WAS
SEATED IN THE BACK
ROW, HE---

Now arrange the circled letters to form
the surprise answer, as suggested by the
above cartoon.

Print
answer
here

# JUMBLE®

Unscramble these four Jumbles, one letter to each square, to form four ordinary words.

UNEES

KALFE

JOADIN

FRIVEY

THE REFEREE THOUGHT THE DEFENSIVE LINEMAN WAS----

Now arrange the circled letters to form the surprise answer, as suggested by the above cartoon.

**Print answer here**

# JUMBLE®

Unscramble these four Jumbles, one letter to each square, to form four ordinary words.

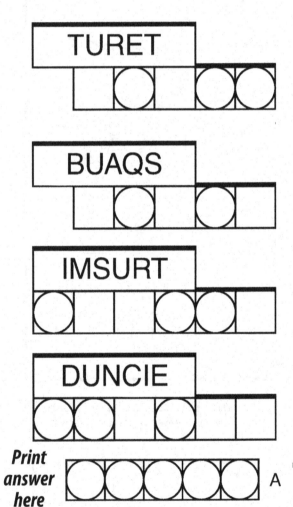

TURET

BUAQS

IMSURT

DUNCIE

Ugh! I can hardly lift this

WHEN THE COOK DRAINED THE HUGE POT OF PASTA, IT WAS----

Now arrange the circled letters to form the surprise answer, as suggested by the above cartoon.

*Print answer here*

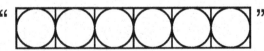

A " "

# JUMBLE®

Unscramble these four Jumbles, one letter to each square, to form four ordinary words.

MOROG

DYRYL

POONUC

VINTEN

I'm starting to sweat

Just a couple more shots

EASY TO BECOME WHEN MODELING FUR COATS.

Now arrange the circled letters to form the surprise answer, as suggested by the above cartoon.

Print answer here A " ⬡⬡⬡⬡⬡ " ⬡⬡⬡⬡

# JUMBLE®

Unscramble these four Jumbles, one letter to
each square, to form four ordinary words.

NUDOM

SBELS

SOLFIS

HEWZEE

I can't afford
a minute's rest

GO NUTS
FOR
DOUGHNUTS

WHEN THE DOUGH-
NUT MAKER BOUGHT
OUT HIS PARTNER,
HE GOT THE ---

Now arrange the circled letters to form
the surprise answer, as suggested by the
above cartoon.

Print
answer
here

" ⬡⬡⬡⬡ "  ⬡⬡⬡⬡⬡⬡⬡⬡⬡

# JUMBLE®

Unscramble these four Jumbles, one letter to each square, to form four ordinary words.

TILUQ

ELTAM

IGGLOO

GNININ

I saw the light!

HOW THE ELEC-
TRICIAN DESCRIBED
THE PREACHER'S
SERMON.

Now arrange the circled letters to form the surprise answer, as suggested by the above cartoon.

Print
answer
here

" ◯◯◯◯◯◯◯◯◯◯◯◯◯ "

# JUMBLE®

Unscramble these four Jumbles, one letter to each square, to form four ordinary words.

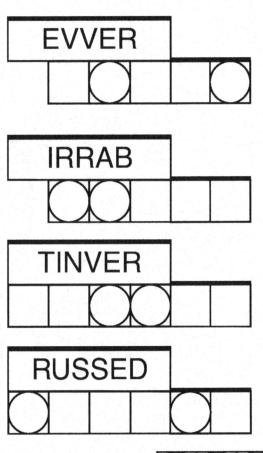

EVVER

IRRAB

TINVER

RUSSED

Where are you going?

I've got to write this down

WHEN THE ASPIRING POET GOT AN IDEA DURING THE NIGHT, HE WENT FROM----

Now arrange the circled letters to form the surprise answer, as suggested by the above cartoon.

*Print answer here*  TO

# JUMBLE®

Unscramble these four Jumbles, one letter to each square, to form four ordinary words.

COVAL

MYRIG

CHINLE

SLUDOH

He's so fast and handsome

THE CHEERLEADER SAID HER BEAU, THE SPRINTER, WAS---

Now arrange the circled letters to form the surprise answer, as suggested by the above cartoon.

*Print answer here* " ◯◯◯◯◯◯◯ "

# JUMBLE®

Unscramble these four Jumbles, one letter to
each square, to form four ordinary words.

RUGPO

SINBO

FOYFAL

UNTEAR

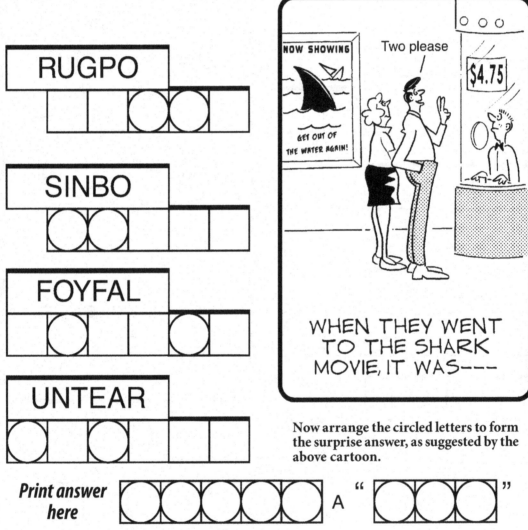

NOW SHOWING

Two please

GET OUT OF
THE WATER AGAIN!

$4.75

WHEN THEY WENT
TO THE SHARK
MOVIE, IT WAS----

Now arrange the circled letters to form
the surprise answer, as suggested by the
above cartoon.

*Print answer
here*          ◯◯◯◯◯ A " ◯◯◯ "

# JUMBLE®

Unscramble these four Jumbles, one letter to each square, to form four ordinary words.

YOBOT

VENAH

LOUTAW

GEXONY

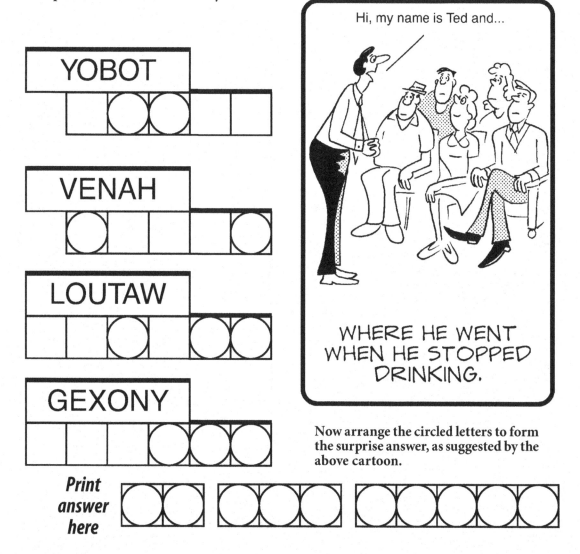

Hi, my name is Ted and...

WHERE HE WENT WHEN HE STOPPED DRINKING.

Now arrange the circled letters to form the surprise answer, as suggested by the above cartoon.

Print answer here

# JUMBLE®

Unscramble these four Jumbles, one letter to
each square, to form four ordinary words.

DRATY

ZABLE

WHARRO

YADLAM

What's in my future?    I love doing this

WHEN THE SEER
READ THEIR
FORTUNE, SHE----

Now arrange the circled letters to form
the surprise answer, as suggested by the
above cartoon.

**Print answer here**  ◯◯◯ A " ◯◯◯◯ "

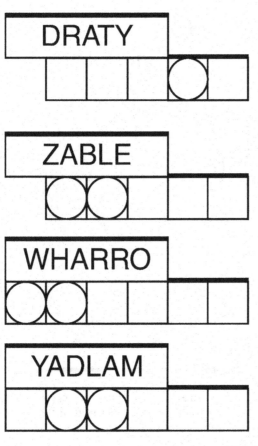

# JUMBLE®

Unscramble these four Jumbles, one letter to
each square, to form four ordinary words.

CENIE

EVVAL

DEMIPE

SHIGLE

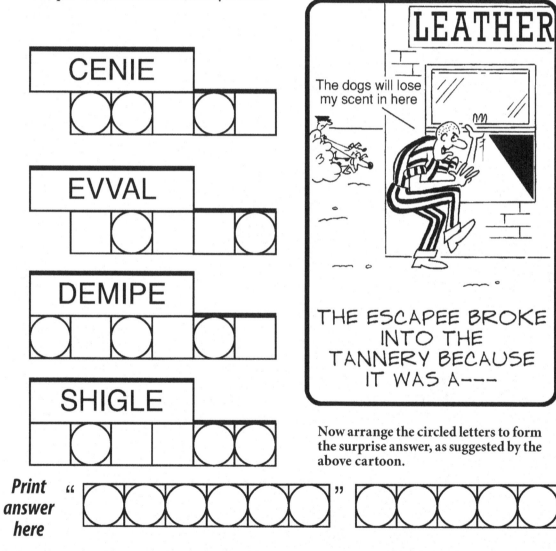

LEATHER

The dogs will lose
my scent in here

THE ESCAPEE BROKE
INTO THE
TANNERY BECAUSE
IT WAS A---

Now arrange the circled letters to form
the surprise answer, as suggested by the
above cartoon.

Print
answer
here   " ⃝⃝⃝⃝⃝⃝ "   ⃝⃝⃝⃝⃝

# JUMBLE®

Unscramble these four Jumbles, one letter to
each square, to form four ordinary words.

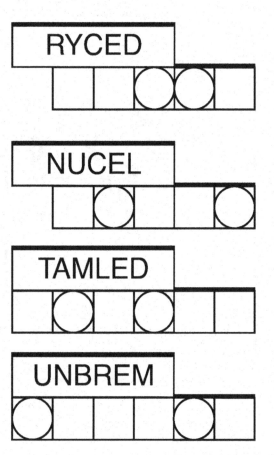

RYCED

NUCEL

TAMLED

UNBREM

Oh, she's lovely

Such poise

A BEAUTY QUEEN
WILL MAKE HER
ENTRANCE TO----

Now arrange the circled letters to form
the surprise answer, as suggested by the
above cartoon.

**Print answer here**

# JUMBLE®

Unscramble these four Jumbles, one letter to each square, to form four ordinary words.

IXTYS

ONLOY

ROTHEY

KHENAS

Jimmy, stop that!

Oh, he's just playing

WHAT THE BOXER DID WHEN HIS GIRL-FRIEND'S LITTLE BROTHER APPEARED.

Now arrange the circled letters to form the surprise answer, as suggested by the above cartoon.

Print answer here

IT ON

# JUMBLE®

Unscramble these four Jumbles, one letter to
each square, to form four ordinary words.

YAASS

GUSET

LADDEY

RACCIT

Oh! I just
had it done

WHEN THE RAIN
RUINED HER
HAIRDO, SHE WAS ---

Now arrange the circled letters to form
the surprise answer, as suggested by the
above cartoon.

Print
answer
here

" ⬡⬡⬡-⬡⬡⬡⬡⬡⬡⬡ "

# JUMBLE®

Unscramble these four Jumbles, one letter to each square, to form four ordinary words.

CEWTI

LODOF

PALLOW

YANNCO

Utilities are extra,
2 months deposit,
no pets

WHAT THE TENANT
GOT WHEN HE RENTED
THE BASEMENT
APARTMENT.

Now arrange the circled letters to form the surprise answer, as suggested by the above cartoon.

*Print answer here* THE " ⬡⬡⬡ - ⬡⬡⬡⬡ "

# JUMBLE.

Unscramble these four Jumbles, one letter to
each square, to form four ordinary words.

STURY

PEROW

MAYGIB

PLECOM

Now what
do we do?

Where are
the oars?

WHEN THE RUNABOUT
STALLED, IT TURNED
INTO A ---

Now arrange the circled letters to form
the surprise answer, as suggested by the
above cartoon.

*Print answer here*   A " ⬡⬡⬡ "  ⬡⬡⬡⬡

# JUMBLE®

Unscramble these four Jumbles, one letter to each square, to form four ordinary words.

CANKS

SYBSA

YURCOT

EVILAB

The cheerleaders are quite lovely

A GOOD WAY TO IMPROVE THE VIEW AT A FOOTBALL GAME,

Now arrange the circled letters to form the surprise answer, as suggested by the above cartoon.

*Print answer here*

# JUMBLE®

Unscramble these four Jumbles, one letter to
each square, to form four ordinary words.

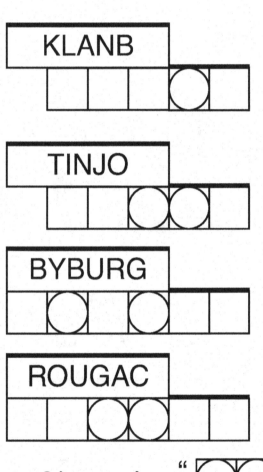

KLANB

TINJO

BYBURG

ROUGAC

I'm going to buy
a bike

FILLING THE GAS
TANK THESE DAYS
CAN LEAVE YOU ----

Now arrange the circled letters to form
the surprise answer, as suggested by the
above cartoon.

Print answer here "  "

82

# JUMBLE®

Unscramble these four Jumbles, one letter to each square, to form four ordinary words.

GWOIN

GLUID

NOPPIL

MOONIK

She's a fine spotter

Look, it's a ...

THE BLUE-EYED BLONDE LED THE BIRD WATCHERS BECAUSE SHE WAS ---

Now arrange the circled letters to form the surprise answer, as suggested by the above cartoon.

Print answer here

" "

# JUMBLE®

Unscramble these four Jumbles, one letter to
each square, to form four ordinary words.

SEPIO

EUQUE

BRYDOW

DAVRIE

I've always
dreamed of a
big wedding

THIS CAN RUIN
A RELATIONSHIP

Now arrange the circled letters to form
the surprise answer, as suggested by the
above cartoon.

Print
answer
here   "◯◯◯◯◯"   ◯◯◯◯◯

# JUMBLE®

Unscramble these four Jumbles, one letter to
each square, to form four ordinary words.

HOCKE

UNGLE

ROTHAX

UNNOIB

Where did
she go?

WHEN THE MAGICIAN
MADE HIS BEAUTIFUL
HELPER DISAPPEAR,
SHE WAS ---

Now arrange the circled letters to form
the surprise answer, as suggested by the
above cartoon.

Print
answer
here

◯◯◯◯◯◯◯ TO ◯◯◯◯ AT

# JUMBLE®

Unscramble these four Jumbles, one letter to
each square, to form four ordinary words.

RAUZE

YLSYH

WURFOR

TUFACE

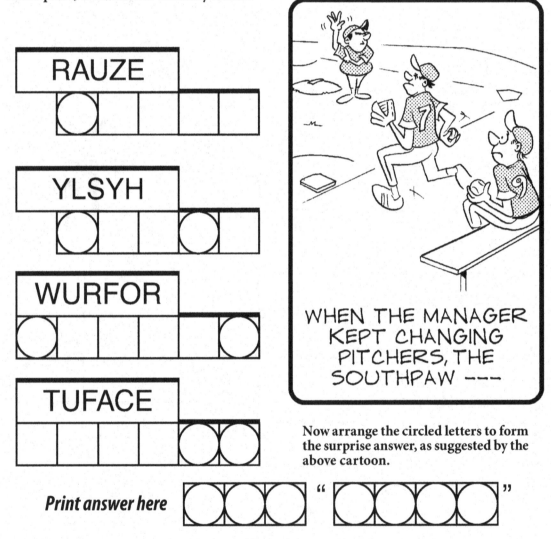

WHEN THE MANAGER
KEPT CHANGING
PITCHERS, THE
SOUTHPAW ---

Now arrange the circled letters to form
the surprise answer, as suggested by the
above cartoon.

*Print answer here*  □○□ " ○○○○ "

# JUMBLE®

Unscramble these four Jumbles, one letter to
each square, to form four ordinary words.

VELGA

PLUIT

SICCUR

IMPAGE

"PIRATES" CAN
GIVE YOU THIS

Now arrange the circled letters to form
the surprise answer, as suggested by the
above cartoon.

*Print answer here*

# JUMBLE®

Unscramble these four Jumbles, one letter to
each square, to form four ordinary words.

LUKKS

RUPOC

HOMIDS

GANTOU

Isn't she
gorgeous?

WHAT THE CAT SHOW
WINNER TURNED
INTO ---

Now arrange the circled letters to form
the surprise answer, as suggested by the
above cartoon.

Print
answer
here    A ◯◯◯◯◯◯◯ " ◯◯◯◯ "

# JUMBLE®

Unscramble these four Jumbles, one letter to each square, to form four ordinary words.

NOBAT

GOFOR

BUHLEM

DARCOW

Are you O.K.?

WHEN THE ICICLE
FELL ON THE
MAILMAN'S HEAD,
HE WAS ---

Now arrange the circled letters to form the surprise answer, as suggested by the above cartoon.

**Print answer here** ◯◯◯ " ◯◯◯◯ "

# JUMBLE®

Unscramble these four Jumbles, one letter to each square, to form four ordinary words.

LOFEN

KEREC

FERREP

NAUVEE

BOOM!

BANG!

Oh, relax

Too much noise!

WHAT THE FEUDING NEIGHBORS HAD ON THE FOURTH OF JULY

Now arrange the circled letters to form the surprise answer, as suggested by the above cartoon.

**Print answer here**   A " ◯◯◯◯◯ "  ◯◯

# JUMBLE®

Unscramble these four Jumbles, one letter to each square, to form four ordinary words.

VARFO

SACEE

JORNAG

VILDER

An ace!
He wins

THE WAITER WON
THE TENNIS MATCH
BECAUSE HE
WAS A ---

Now arrange the circled letters to form the surprise answer, as suggested by the above cartoon.

*Print answer here*  "          "

# JUMBLE®

Unscramble these four Jumbles, one letter to
each square, to form four ordinary words.

TANCE

TUFLE

BOYDEM

LOWHYL

He doesn't waste
any time

WHEN THE OLD–TIME
TELEGRAPH
OPERATOR SENT HIS
HOURLY MESSAGE,
IT WAS———

Now arrange the circled letters to form
the surprise answer, as suggested by the
above cartoon.

**Print answer here**   ON ⬡⬡⬡ " ⬡⬡⬡ "

# JUMBLE®

Unscramble these four Jumbles, one letter to each square, to form four ordinary words.

RILCY

TEYIP

ORFALL

INSEPP

I'm playing a sneaky character

THE ACTOR USED GREASEPAINT BECAUSE HE HAD A ---

Now arrange the circled letters to form the surprise answer, as suggested by the above cartoon.

Print answer here

"⭕⭕⭕⭕⭕⭕⭕⭕" ⭕⭕⭕⭕

93

# JUMBLE®

Unscramble these four Jumbles, one letter to
each square, to form four ordinary words.

TAFAL

ADDEJ

CLINEY

TRAVOC

Maybe we shouldn't
get married

Don't tell me
how to drive!

WHEN HER FIANCE
GOT HOT UNDER
THE COLLAR, SHE
ENDED UP WITH ---

Now arrange the circled letters to form
the surprise answer, as suggested by the
above cartoon.

*Print answer here*

# JUMBLE®

Unscramble these four Jumbles, one letter to
each square, to form four ordinary words.

CAPHO

STATY

DASSIT

SAMIPH

He embezzled
bank funds

THE CONVICT
ENJOYED SITTING
IN THE SUN BECAUSE
HE HAD A ---

Now arrange the circled letters to form
the surprise answer, as suggested by the
above cartoon.

Print answer " ⬡⬡⬡⬡⬡ " ⬡⬡⬡⬡
here

# JUMBLE®

Unscramble these four Jumbles, one letter to
each square, to form four ordinary words.

TOROB

TEQUS

ZERTHI

ACNIPT

You belong in
this beauty

Can I have your
autograph?

WHEN THE
EX-STRIKEOUT
KING SOLD CARS,
HE USED HIS ----

Now arrange the circled letters to form
the surprise answer, as suggested by the
above cartoon.

**Print answer
here**  ◯◯◯◯ " ◯◯◯◯◯ "

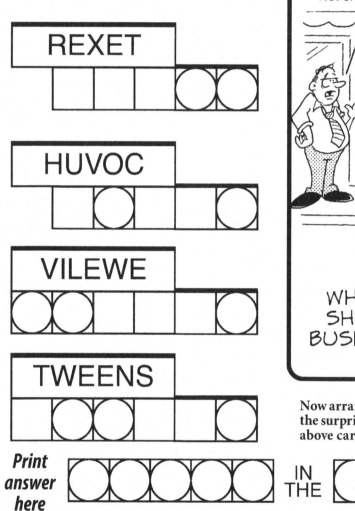

# JUMBLE®

Unscramble these four Jumbles, one letter to each square, to form four ordinary words.

REXET

HUVOC

VILEWE

TWEENS

Not enough business

CLOSING SALE

SALE

10
DAYS
LEFT

WHAT THE BATH
SHOP DID WHEN
BUSINESS SOURED

Now arrange the circled letters to form the surprise answer, as suggested by the above cartoon.

Print
answer
here

IN
THE

# JUMBLE®

Unscramble these four Jumbles, one letter to each square, to form four ordinary words.

EXVIN

NAYGO

YOMFID

LAFBLE

Guilty!
$50.00.
Next!

FOR A TRAFFIC
COURT JUDGE, IT'S
ALWAYS A ---

Now arrange the circled letters to form the surprise answer, as suggested by the above cartoon.

**Print answer here** "⬡⬡⬡⬡" ⬡⬡⬡

# JUMBLE®

Unscramble these four Jumbles, one letter to
each square, to form four ordinary words.

GEBOF

BODUT

CONARY

ENGOBY

Do I hear
$2,500?

That's enough.
Let's go

WHAT HE BID
AT THE AUCTION

Now arrange the circled letters to form
the surprise answer, as suggested by the
above cartoon.

**Print answer here**

# JUMBLE®

Unscramble these four Jumbles, one letter to
each square, to form four ordinary words.

KANTE

UMPEL

UNMOLC

DINCUT

The saw is stuck again

You're through!

THE CARPENTER
FIRED HIS HELPER
BECAUSE HE ----

Now arrange the circled letters to form
the surprise answer, as suggested by the
above cartoon.

Print
answer
here

◯◯◯◯◯◯ ' ◯ " ◯◯◯ " IT

# JUMBLE®

Unscramble these four Jumbles, one letter to
each square, to form four ordinary words.

GNUST

SHIWK

UNMUTA

PORTIM

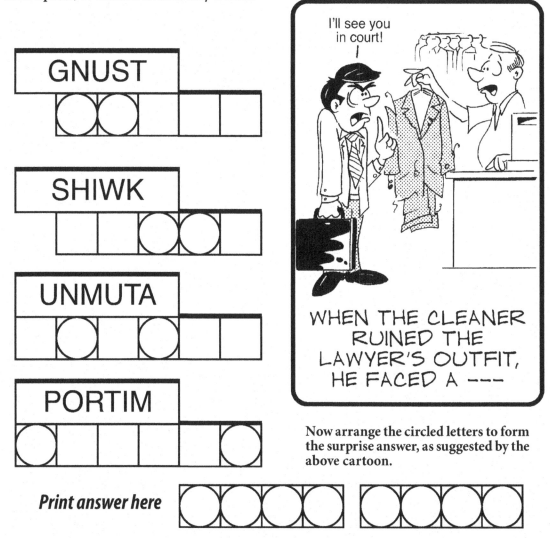

I'll see you
in court!

WHEN THE CLEANER
RUINED THE
LAWYER'S OUTFIT,
HE FACED A ----

Now arrange the circled letters to form
the surprise answer, as suggested by the
above cartoon.

**Print answer here**

# JUMBLE®

Unscramble these four Jumbles, one letter to each square, to form four ordinary words.

VOABE

HOTOT

RUPALL

ATTARR

You're three hours late

EASY TO GET
WITHOUT A LOT
OF TROUBLE

Now arrange the circled letters to form the surprise answer, as suggested by the above cartoon.

Print answer here    A ◯◯◯ OF ◯◯◯◯◯◯◯

# JUMBLE®

Unscramble these four Jumbles, one letter to each square, to form four ordinary words.

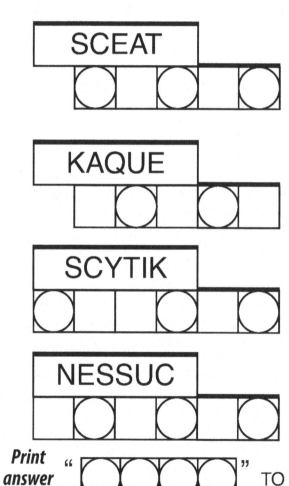

SCEAT

KAQUE

SCYTIK

NESSUC

What concentration

His hands
are magical

WHEN THE CONCERT
PIANIST PERFORMED
HE EXHIBITED
HIS ---

Now arrange the circled letters to form the surprise answer, as suggested by the above cartoon.

**Print answer here** " ◯◯◯◯ " TO ◯◯◯◯◯◯◯

# JUMBLE®

Unscramble these four Jumbles, one letter to each square, to form four ordinary words.

POASY

PHULS

DUPLED

ZARBLE

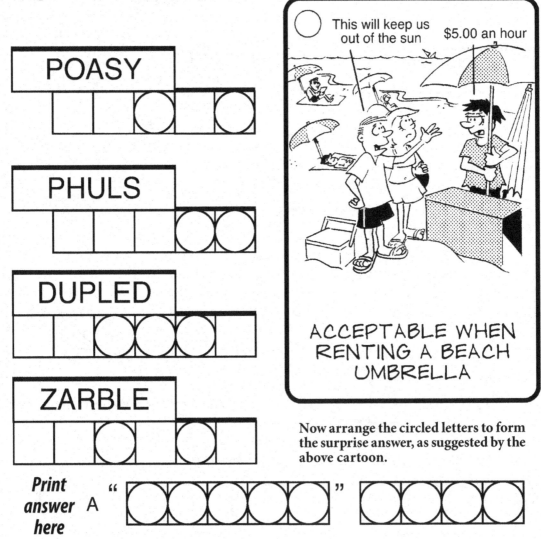

This will keep us out of the sun

$5.00 an hour

ACCEPTABLE WHEN RENTING A BEACH UMBRELLA

Now arrange the circled letters to form the surprise answer, as suggested by the above cartoon.

Print answer here    A " ⬡⬡⬡⬡⬡ "  ⬡⬡⬡⬡

# JUMBLE®

Unscramble these four Jumbles, one letter to
each square, to form four ordinary words.

PLONY

VENIG

FLUNIX

WINDOS

You're hired.
Cover that up

DONE BY A
LABORER WHEN
HE GETS THE JOB

Now arrange the circled letters to form
the surprise answer, as suggested by the
above cartoon.

Print
answer
here
THE " "

# JUMBLE®

Unscramble these four Jumbles, one letter to
each square, to form four ordinary words.

IMPER

FARCT

SPICET

TUITOW

My husband is
so interesting

SHE MARRIED A
NOVELIST BECAUSE
HE WAS ---

Now arrange the circled letters to form
the surprise answer, as suggested by the
above cartoon.

*Print
answer
here*

"           "

# JUMBLE®

Unscramble these four Jumbles, one letter to
each square, to form four ordinary words.

CHUGO

LOCCI

TADWYR

VAHLIS

That's all
I've got.
Keep the clip.

WHAT THE TYCOON
RESORTED TO
WHEN HIS ASSETS
WERE FROZEN

Now arrange the circled letters to form
the surprise answer, as suggested by the
above cartoon.

*Print answer here*

# JUMBLE®

Unscramble these four Jumbles, one letter to
each square, to form four ordinary words.

**DAMMA**

**UGGEA**

**LENKER**

**BRUBRE**

Wow!
She's gorgeous

She won't give
you the time of day

ALTHOUGH SHE
WAS STUCK-UP, HER
LOOKS MADE HIM ---

Now arrange the circled letters to form
the surprise answer, as suggested by the
above cartoon.

**Print answer here** " ◯◯◯◯◯◯◯ "

# JUMBLE®

Unscramble these four Jumbles, one letter to each square, to form four ordinary words.

TELLU

FARCS

ORSOUP

AHNRAG

Get whatever you want

WHAT SHE GOT WHEN THE SUGAR DADDY GAVE HER HIS CREDIT CARD

Now arrange the circled letters to form the surprise answer, as suggested by the above cartoon.

Print answer here

A " ◯◯◯◯◯◯ " ◯◯◯ ◯◯ IT

# JUMBLE®

Unscramble these four Jumbles, one letter to each square, to form four ordinary words.

NORCO

YACKT

RAFIAN

LARBUT

Good mileage, 5-year warranty and ...

Can we afford it?

THIS TAKES SOME STUDY BEFORE A BIG PURCHASE

Now arrange the circled letters to form the surprise answer, as suggested by the above cartoon.

Print answer here

A

# JUMBLE®

Unscramble these four Jumbles, one letter to each square, to form four ordinary words.

DRUFA

MYPUB

PERUSH

NUTJAY

Is he available?

He looks married

WHAT A SINGLE GIRL SHOULDN'T LOOK FOR WHEN SHE'S LOOKING FOR THIS

Now arrange the circled letters to form the surprise answer, as suggested by the above cartoon.

**Print answer here** A ◯◯◯◯◯◯◯

# JUMBLE®

Unscramble these four Jumbles, one letter to each square, to form four ordinary words.

AVUME

NEMOD

TEENIC

WHAIGE

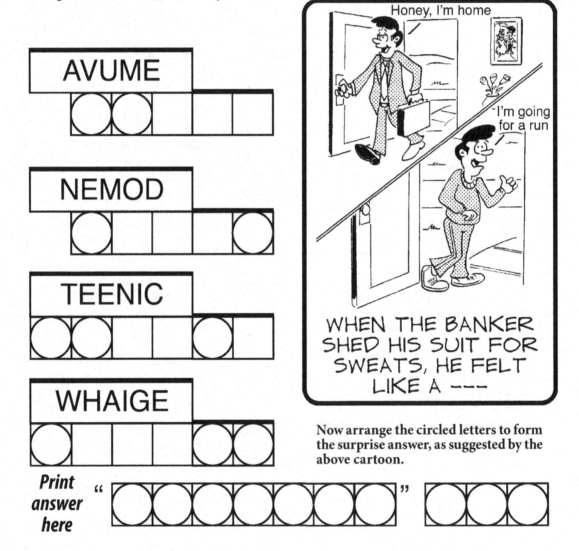

Honey, I'm home

I'm going for a run

WHEN THE BANKER SHED HIS SUIT FOR SWEATS, HE FELT LIKE A ---

Now arrange the circled letters to form the surprise answer, as suggested by the above cartoon.

Print answer here

"⬭⬭⬭⬭⬭⬭⬭" ⬭⬭⬭

# JUMBLE

Unscramble these four Jumbles, one letter to each square, to form four ordinary words.

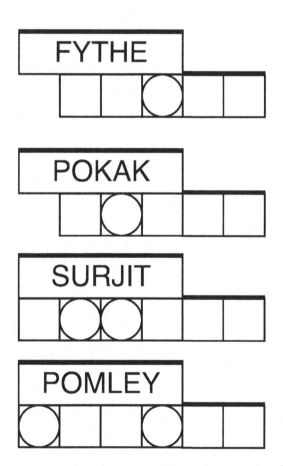

FYTHE

POKAK

SURJIT

POMLEY

Don't tell anyone, but Marge is ...

WHAT A MOUTHFUL OF GOSSIP CAN RESULT IN

Now arrange the circled letters to form the surprise answer, as suggested by the above cartoon.

*Print answer here* AN

# JUMBLE®

Unscramble these four Jumbles, one letter to each square, to form four ordinary words.

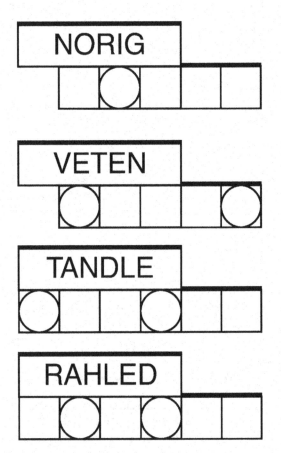

NORIG

VETEN

TANDLE

RAHLED

WHEN THE DOCTOR DIDN'T CHARGE HIM, THE YOUNG PATIENT WAS ---

Now arrange the circled letters to form the surprise answer, as suggested by the above cartoon.

Print answer here "  "

# JUMBLE®

Unscramble these four Jumbles, one letter to
each square, to form four ordinary words.

MYDUP

PUMIO

LAWHOL

NOYKED

You're the
best player

Can we have
your autograph?

WHAT THE SCHOOL-
BOYS DID WHEN
THEY MET THE
BASKETBALL STAR

Now arrange the circled letters to form
the surprise answer, as suggested by the
above cartoon.

Print
answer
here

"    " TO

# JUMBLE®

Unscramble these four Jumbles, one letter to
each square, to form four ordinary words.

NELLK

CRAID

LUWANT

LIKALA

He's the runaway
favorite

VOTE!

CARL for MAYOR

HOW THE BAKER
WON THE TOWN
ELECTION

Now arrange the circled letters to form
the surprise answer, as suggested by the
above cartoon.

**Print
answer
here**   A

# JUMBLE®

Unscramble these four Jumbles, one letter to
each square, to form four ordinary words.

NACEP

THACC

HOIDAR

FEXPIR

Here's our honeymoon suite

WHAT THE GROOM
DID WHEN HE
MARRIED THE
MATH TEACHER

Now arrange the circled letters to form
the surprise answer, as suggested by the
above cartoon.

Print
answer
here

THE " "

# JUMBLE®

Unscramble these four Jumbles, one letter to
each square, to form four ordinary words.

HIFAT

APROV

DOUSEX

NAHDDE

This is a big job          Call someone

THE OWNER DIDN'T
REPAIR THE ROOF
BECAUSE IT WAS ----

Now arrange the circled letters to form
the surprise answer, as suggested by the
above cartoon.

Print
answer
here

# JUMBLE®

Unscramble these four Jumbles, one letter to
each square, to form four ordinary words.

KHYAS

RAOAM

YOUCTH

MEEGUL

THE KIND OF DRESS
WORN BY A GHOST

Now arrange the circled letters to form
the surprise answer, as suggested by the
above cartoon.

*Print
answer
here*

⬡⬡⬡ - ⬡⬡⬡⬡⬡⬡⬡⬡

# JUMBLE®

Unscramble these four Jumbles, one letter to each square, to form four ordinary words.

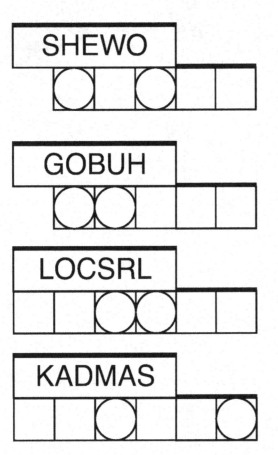

SHEWO

GOBUH

LOCSRL

KADMAS

Ask him. He reads everything

Do you know of a good mystery?

FICTION

INFORMATION

WHAT HE USED WHEN HE WAS FISHING FOR A GOOD NOVEL

Now arrange the circled letters to form the surprise answer, as suggested by the above cartoon.

Print answer here    A

120

# JUMBLE®

Unscramble these four Jumbles, one letter to
each square, to form four ordinary words.

DROUG

MALUB

REVEWS

PHEPOR

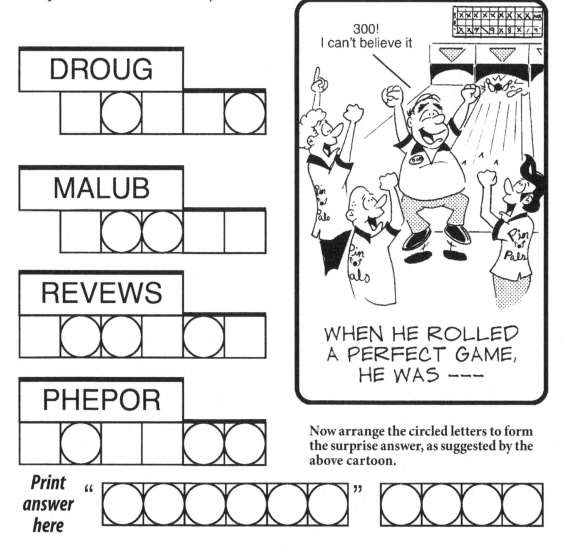

300!
I can't believe it

WHEN HE ROLLED
A PERFECT GAME,
HE WAS ---

Now arrange the circled letters to form
the surprise answer, as suggested by the
above cartoon.

Print
answer
here   " ◯◯◯◯◯◯ "   ◯◯◯◯

# JUMBLE®

Unscramble these four Jumbles, one letter to each square, to form four ordinary words.

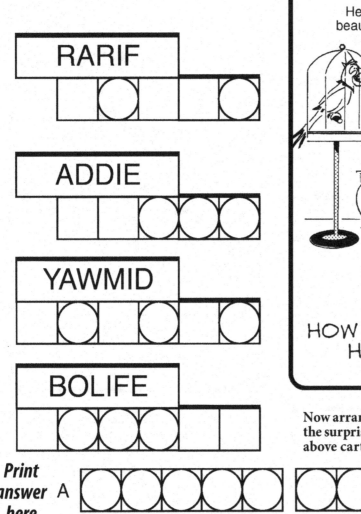

RARIF

ADDIE

YAWMID

BOLIFE

Hello you beautiful doll

AAWK

He has quite a vocabulary

HOW HE DESCRIBED HIS PARROT

Now arrange the circled letters to form the surprise answer, as suggested by the above cartoon.

*Print answer here* A

# JUMBLE®

Unscramble these four Jumbles, one letter to
each square, to form four ordinary words.

ZAWLT

HYDUC

INDAGE

SIMREY

They're biting
by the weeds

This will make
good eating

WHERE YOU CAN
FIND THE
MOST FISH

Now arrange the circled letters to form
the surprise answer, as suggested by the
above cartoon.

*Print answer
here*   IN

123

# JUMBLE®

Unscramble these four Jumbles, one letter to each square, to form four ordinary words.

BIMOL

HELEW

DIPSUT

DELBOH

Perfect. Nice job

Here's the final total

WHEN THEIR HOUSE WAS COMPLETED, THE COUPLE WAS ---

Now arrange the circled letters to form the surprise answer, as suggested by the above cartoon.

*Print answer here*

# JUMBLE®

Unscramble these four Jumbles, one letter to each square, to form four ordinary words.

UPYTT

SLARN

NOCABE

KABETS

Just a temporary
market adjustment

My portfolio
is down 15%

WHAT THE BROKER
GAVE THE NERVOUS
INVESTOR

Now arrange the circled letters to form the surprise answer, as suggested by the above cartoon.

Print
answer
here

A " ⬤⬤⬤⬤⬤ " ⬤⬤⬤⬤⬤

# JUMBLE®

Unscramble these four Jumbles, one letter to each square, to form four ordinary words.

WHASA

VEYHA

MOONID

NERVAG

This may help someone live

GIVE BLOOD

SUE

A DEPOSIT AT THE BLOOD BANK IS A ---

Now arrange the circled letters to form the surprise answer, as suggested by the above cartoon.

Print answer here

☐☐☐☐☐ ☐☐☐ TO " ☐☐☐☐ "

# JUMBLE®

Unscramble these four Jumbles, one letter to
each square, to form four ordinary words.

KLAYB

ZIPER

UNBRAU

SHARTH

You weren't
here last
week

Sure
I was

WHAT THE GARBAGE
MAN SAID WHEN THE
CUSTOMER
COMPLAINED

Now arrange the circled letters to form
the surprise answer, as suggested by the
above cartoon.

**Print answer here** "  "

127

# JUMBLE®

Unscramble these four Jumbles, one letter to each square, to form four ordinary words.

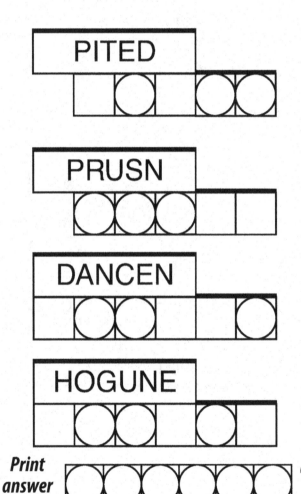

PITED

PRUSN

DANCEN

HOGUNE

Here's my bill

Wonderful.
I've lost another
ten

WHAT THE DIETITIAN
DID WHEN THE
ENGLISH PATIENT
LOST WEIGHT

Now arrange the circled letters to form the surprise answer, as suggested by the above cartoon.

**Print answer here**

# JUMBLE®

Unscramble these four Jumbles, one letter to each square, to form four ordinary words.

NOAPI

LIGUT

INCANE

SYMFLE

How 'bout another, ol' pal?

Don't mind if I do

THIS CAN MAKE FOR A "GENIAL" EVENING

Now arrange the circled letters to form the surprise answer, as suggested by the above cartoon.

*Print answer here* ⬡⬡⬡ AND ⬡⬡⬡

# JUMBLE

Unscramble these four Jumbles, one letter to
each square, to form four ordinary words.

**ERQUE**

**TEPIN**

**HECARB**

**EMTYSS**

This is a good
place to discuss
personnel

WHAT THE
EXECUTIVES NEEDED
WHEN THEY MET
FOR A BITE ---

Now arrange the circled letters to form
the surprise answer, as suggested by the
above cartoon.

**Print answer here**

# JUMBLE®

Unscramble these four Jumbles, one letter to each square, to form four ordinary words.

HORAB

MUBIE

LAROSI

TENJIC

You need to look your best today

THE GROOMER BRUSHED THE SHOW HORSE'S HAIR BECAUSE IT WAS ----

Now arrange the circled letters to form the surprise answer, as suggested by the above cartoon.

Print answer here

" "

# JUMBLE®

Unscramble these four Jumbles, one letter to
each square, to form four ordinary words.

ENNIL

ROHNO

NICKES

POATTE

It's a sound
investment

NEEDED WHEN
BUYING AND PLAYING
A VINTAGE VIOLIN

Now arrange the circled letters to form
the surprise answer, as suggested by the
above cartoon.

*Print answer here* "  "

# JUMBLE®

Unscramble these four Jumbles, one letter to each square, to form four ordinary words.

**ADNUT**

**ECHLE**

**BOWELL**

**DARFOE**

I've gained another five pounds

TOO MANY SQUARE MEALS CAN MAKE ONE ---

Now arrange the circled letters to form the surprise answer, as suggested by the above cartoon.

*Print answer here*

" "

# JUMBLE ®

Unscramble these four Jumbles, one letter to
each square, to form four ordinary words.

RINPT

VANKE

STRAIG

SATHAG

It took forever
to find it

It's perfect

WHAT THE COUPLE
WENT THROUGH
BUYING THE RIGHT
HOUSE

Now arrange the circled letters to form
the surprise answer, as suggested by the
above cartoon.

Print
answer
here

# JUMBLE®

Unscramble these four Jumbles, one letter to each square, to form four ordinary words.

**GEREM**

**TUNYT**

**GISMOE**

**MAJEST**

What a sight

HOW THE COUPLE DESCRIBED THE GRAND CANYON

Now arrange the circled letters to form the surprise answer, as suggested by the above cartoon.

Print answer here

" "

# JUMBLE®

Unscramble these four Jumbles, one letter to each square, to form four ordinary words.

FARIE

TYDIT

SULUFE

ARPITE

Watch out for stumps

Oops!

WHAT THE SCOUT EXPERIENCED WHEN HE HIKED THROUGH THE WOODS

Now arrange the circled letters to form the surprise answer, as suggested by the above cartoon.

Print answer here    A ◯◯◯◯◯ " ◯◯◯◯ "

# JUMBLE®

Unscramble these four Jumbles, one letter to each square, to form four ordinary words.

POREA

NAJOB

BRATIL

WABUSY

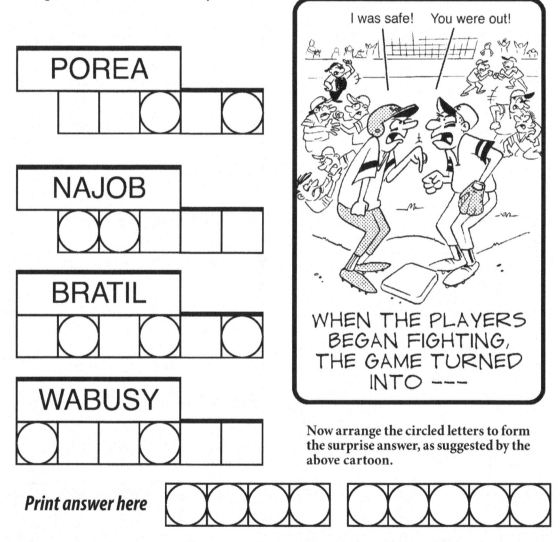

I was safe!   You were out!

WHEN THE PLAYERS BEGAN FIGHTING, THE GAME TURNED INTO ---

Now arrange the circled letters to form the surprise answer, as suggested by the above cartoon.

**Print answer here**

# JUMBLE®

Unscramble these four Jumbles, one letter to each square, to form four ordinary words.

NESOO

SPEHE

TRIEHD

TUVIRE

ON YOUR FEET!
Your boots are filthy

WHAT THE SARGE
SAID TO THE
SLEEPING RECRUIT

Now arrange the circled letters to form the surprise answer, as suggested by the above cartoon.

*Print answer here*  ⬚⬚⬚⬚ AND ⬚⬚⬚⬚⬚

# JUMBLE®

Unscramble these four Jumbles, one letter to
each square, to form four ordinary words.

**PUJMY**

**HUTEC**

**UPVERY**

**GENJAL**

What a lovely.
presentation

I'm starved

NO MATTER WHAT
IS SERVED, THIS WILL
MAKE IT ATTRACTIVE.

Now arrange the circled letters to form
the surprise answer, as suggested by the
above cartoon.

*Print answer here*

# JUMBLE®

Unscramble these four Jumbles, one letter to
each square, to form four ordinary words.

ASTEE

CYRUR

PORTSY

USDABE

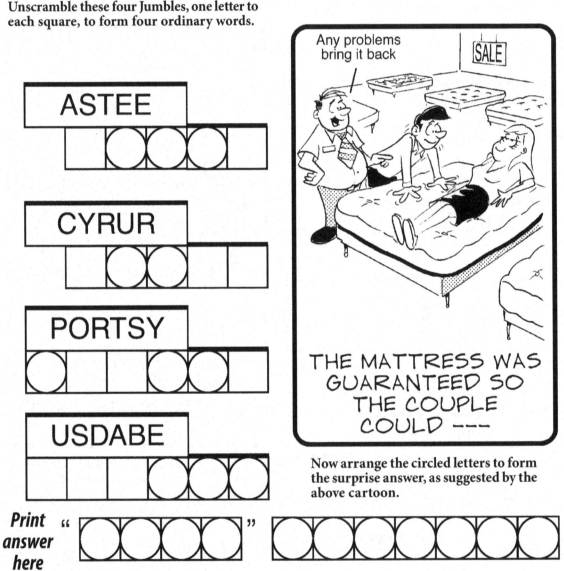

Any problems
bring it back

SALE

THE MATTRESS WAS
GUARANTEED SO
THE COUPLE
COULD ----

Now arrange the circled letters to form
the surprise answer, as suggested by the
above cartoon.

Print
answer
here

" ⬡⬡⬡⬡ "  ⬡⬡⬡⬡⬡⬡⬡⬡

# JUMBLE®

Unscramble these four Jumbles, one letter to each square, to form four ordinary words.

PLITO

ROGGE

PRUMBE

SUDSIC

It looks so real.
I love it

OOTTAT
-N-

WHEN THE TATTOO ARTIST PUT A BUTTERFLY ON HER LEG, SHE WAS ----

Now arrange the circled letters to form the surprise answer, as suggested by the above cartoon.

Print answer here " _____ "

# JUMBLE®

Unscramble these four Jumbles, one letter to
each square, to form four ordinary words.

HOACC

FREVE

SEPORC

TERLIP

Come with me, cowboy

SALOON

WHAT THE SHERIFF
ALWAYS HAS IN A
WESTERN MOVIE.

Now arrange the circled letters to form
the surprise answer, as suggested by the
above cartoon.

Print answer
here      A "⃝⃝⃝⃝⃝"  ⃝⃝⃝⃝

# JUMBLE®

Unscramble these four Jumbles, one letter to each square, to form four ordinary words.

EBELL

IXAMM

DICLAP

VITANY

Beats me

Royal Flush!

EVEN A KING TAKES
A BACK SEAT TO THIS
IN A POKER GAME.

Now arrange the circled letters to form the surprise answer, as suggested by the above cartoon.

*Print answer here* ⬡⬡ ⬡⬡⬡

# JUMBLE®

Unscramble these four Jumbles, one letter to
each square, to form four ordinary words.

WADAR

LAANB

CLUSKE

DACUDE

This isn't as easy
as it looks

WHEN HE TRIED HIS
HAND AT ARCHERY,
HE DISCOVERED
IT HAD ———

Now arrange the circled letters to form
the surprise answer, as suggested by the
above cartoon.

Print answer "⬡⬡⬡⬡⬡⬡⬡⬡⬡"
here

# JUMBLE®

Unscramble these four Jumbles, one letter to
each square, to form four ordinary words.

APANG

OCTIX

TIBESC

HYFORT

Don't "my dear" me

Good evening,
my dear

HOW A NIGHT
ON THE TOWN
LEFT HIM.

Now arrange the circled letters to form
the surprise answer, as suggested by the
above cartoon.

Print
answer
here

IN A "◯◯◯◯◯" ◯◯◯◯

# JUMBLE®

Unscramble these four Jumbles, one letter to each square, to form four ordinary words.

YOPPP

OPSOW

TOATER

GLINTE

C'mon! Get with it

WHAT A PHOTO-GRAPHER CAN DO WITH A BORED MODEL.

Now arrange the circled letters to form the surprise answer, as suggested by the above cartoon.

**Print answer here** " "

146

# JUMBLE®

Unscramble these four Jumbles, one letter to each square, to form four ordinary words.

CEEPA

CLATH

FIMITS

LEPHER

MEOW
SCREECH
The cats are fighting again

IN FOR DINNER, BUT FREQUENTLY OUT ALL NIGHT.

Now arrange the circled letters to form the surprise answer, as suggested by the above cartoon.

Print answer here

147

# JUMBLE®

Unscramble these four Jumbles, one letter to each square, to form four ordinary words.

SIONE

SNAPY

MYSLOB

LETTEK

First we work on posture, then on rhythm, then...

WHAT IT TAKES TO BECOME A BALLROOM DANCER.

Now arrange the circled letters to form the surprise answer, as suggested by the above cartoon.

Print answer here

☐☐☐☐ OF " ☐☐☐☐☐ "

# JUMBLE®

Unscramble these four Jumbles, one letter to
each square, to form four ordinary words.

MYLAN

ALLEG

RILIXE

EXCOBI

STEE-RIKE

Of all the dumb...
Are you blind?

WHEN THE MANAGER
LET OFF STEAM,
HE WAS ---

Now arrange the circled letters to form
the surprise answer, as suggested by the
above cartoon.

**Print answer here** " ◯◯◯◯◯◯◯◯ "

# JUMBLE®

Unscramble these four Jumbles, one letter to each square, to form four ordinary words.

BYNAD

LITEE

EMFLEA

CAUTAL

Has it ever snowed here?

IT DOESN'T EXIST AT THE EQUATOR.

Now arrange the circled letters to form the surprise answer, as suggested by the above cartoon.

**Print answer here**

# JUMBLE®

Unscramble these four Jumbles, one letter to each square, to form four ordinary words.

MEERB

LYAID

JONNIE

BAILUR

You weren't straight with us

WHEN HE CROSSED THE COPS, THE STOOL PIGEON BECAME A ---

Now arrange the circled letters to form the surprise answer, as suggested by the above cartoon.

*Print answer here*

# JUMBLE®

Unscramble these four Jumbles, one letter to
each square, to form four ordinary words.

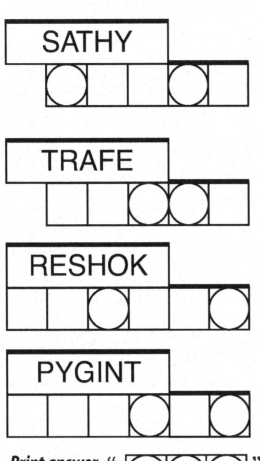

SATHY

TRAFE

RESHOK

PYGINT

You need a
short curly look

WHAT THE HAIR-
DRESSER DID FOR
THE LONG-HAIRED
BRUNETTE.

Now arrange the circled letters to form
the surprise answer, as suggested by the
above cartoon.

Print answer " ◯◯◯ " HER ◯◯◯◯◯
here

152

# JUMBLE®

Unscramble these four Jumbles, one letter to each square, to form four ordinary words.

**MUNAH**

**GEDEW**

**NETEOD**

**REYHEB**

Dig it.
Plant it.
Do it again.

THE FARMER'S
SIMPLE PHILOSOPHY
WAS ---

Now arrange the circled letters to form the surprise answer, as suggested by the above cartoon.

*Print answer here*  ⬡⬡⬡⬡ TO " ⬡⬡⬡⬡⬡ "

# JUMBLE®

Unscramble these four Jumbles, one letter to
each square, to form four ordinary words.

KWONN

HITEL

ROQUIL

THUGOR

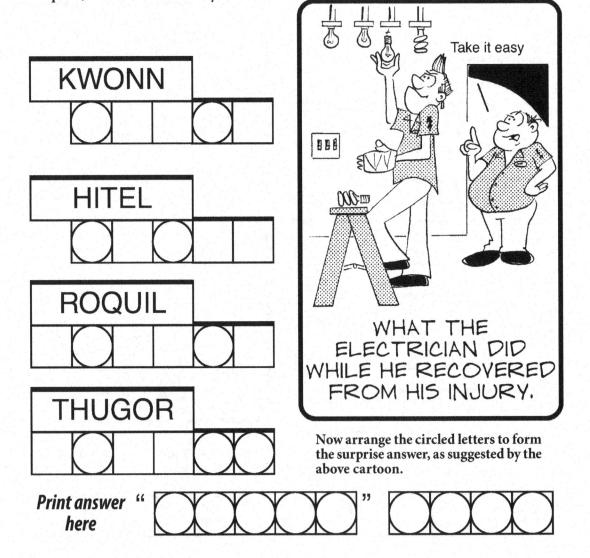

Take it easy

WHAT THE
ELECTRICIAN DID
WHILE HE RECOVERED
FROM HIS INJURY.

Now arrange the circled letters to form
the surprise answer, as suggested by the
above cartoon.

*Print answer
here* " ◯◯◯◯◯ " ◯◯◯◯

# JUMBLE®

Unscramble these four Jumbles, one letter to each square, to form four ordinary words.

TACHY

TIDIO

BABFLY

TEMRIP

I enjoy spending time with you

He could be the one

WHEN THEY MET ON HORSEBACK, SHE WAS ON THE ---

Now arrange the circled letters to form the surprise answer, as suggested by the above cartoon.

Print answer here

" ⃝⃝⃝⃝⃝⃝ "  ⃝⃝⃝⃝

# JUMBLE®

Unscramble these four Jumbles, one letter to
each square, to form four ordinary words.

TUINY

SOSBA

RECLEY

LEMITY

He's been studying
for years

THE MAILMAN RECEIVED
AN ADVANCED
DEGREE BECAUSE
HE WAS A ---

Now arrange the circled letters to form
the surprise answer, as suggested by the
above cartoon.

Print
answer
here ⬡⬡⬡ OF " ⬡⬡⬡⬡⬡⬡⬡⬡ "

156

# JUMBLE®

Unscramble these four Jumbles, one letter to each square, to form four ordinary words.

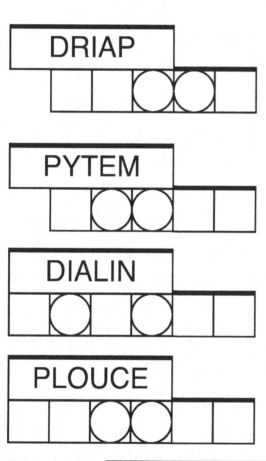

DRIAP

PYTEM

DIALIN

PLOUCE

STREET FESTIVAL

My foot is killing me

POI

WHAT SHE EXPERIENCED WHEN SHE DANCED IN HER NEW SHOES.

Now arrange the circled letters to form the surprise answer, as suggested by the above cartoon.

**Print answer here**

 AT THE "  "

157

# JUMBLE®

Unscramble these four Jumbles, one letter to
each square, to form four ordinary words.

**DUPON**

**DALIP**

**HUCNAH**

**FEWLOU**

They're trying
to catch the
bank robbers

What's the delay?

THE POLICE
ROADBLOCK
LED TO A ---

Now arrange the circled letters to form
the surprise answer, as suggested by the
above cartoon.

**Print
answer
here**

# JUMBLE®

Unscramble these four Jumbles, one letter to
each square, to form four ordinary words.

PLUJE

ACOME

RUPPLE

BOTERD

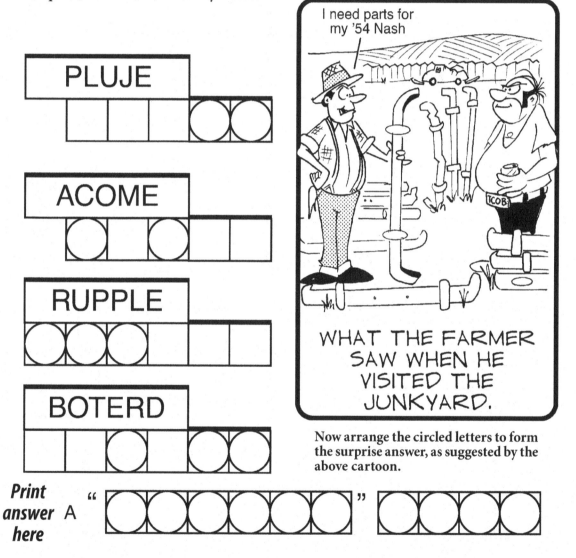

I need parts for
my '54 Nash

WHAT THE FARMER
SAW WHEN HE
VISITED THE
JUNKYARD.

Now arrange the circled letters to form
the surprise answer, as suggested by the
above cartoon.

Print
answer    A    "⎵⎵⎵⎵⎵⎵"    ⎵⎵⎵⎵
here

# JUMBLE®

Unscramble these four Jumbles, one letter to each square, to form four ordinary words.

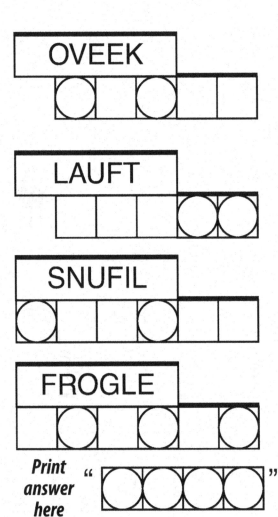

OVEEK

LAUFT

SNUFIL

FROGLE

He's handsome and he's building another subdivision

SHE CHASED THE REAL ESTATE DEVELOPER BECAUSE HE HAD ---

Now arrange the circled letters to form the surprise answer, as suggested by the above cartoon.

Print answer here " ⃝⃝⃝⃝ " TO ⃝⃝⃝⃝⃝

# JUMBLE®

Unscramble these four Jumbles, one letter to
each square, to form four ordinary words.

LEKAN

TIHHC

KRAYBE

NITTEK

Hey, good looking.
Going my way?

WHAT SHE THOUGHT
WHEN THEIR PATHS
CROSSED ON
THE TRAIL.

Now arrange the circled letters to form
the surprise answer, as suggested by the
above cartoon.

**Print answer here**

 A

161

# JUMBLE®

Unscramble these four Jumbles, one letter to each square, to form four ordinary words.

NILOG

ARROD

RINMAT

LENKEN

I thought we were going out

Ball game's on

WISE TO DO WHEN IT'S "LOVE AT FIRST SIGHT."

Now arrange the circled letters to form the surprise answer, as suggested by the above cartoon.

*Print answer here*

# JUMBLE®

# Vacation

## Challenger Puzzles

# JUMBLE

Unscramble these six Jumbles, one letter to
each square, to form six ordinary words.

CYMALL

INGOHM

BLACOT

LESFAT

DISNAL

EHLTMA

Mostly B's.
The tutor really
helped

CLASS of 2005

WHAT IT TOOK
TO GET HIS SON
THROUGH COLLEGE

Now arrange the circled letters to form
the surprise answer, as suggested by
the above cartoon.

**Print answer here**

HE

# JUMBLE®

Unscramble these six Jumbles, one letter to each square, to form six ordinary words.

LAPPOR

DEELMY

RAUBUE

BREMME

DEHEAB

JEDGAG

He counterfeits
$100 bills

THE CROOKED
BAKER WAS ARRESTED
FOR ---

Now arrange the circled letters to form the surprise answer, as suggested by the above cartoon.

**Print answer here**

◯◯◯◯◯◯◯◯ " ◯◯◯◯◯ "

# JUMBLE®

Unscramble these six Jumbles, one letter to
each square, to form six ordinary words.

CYGERL

TALLEM

REBOOL

DESSUR

CAHBLE

OSMACT

You all look lovely

404

It's so
boring

Same outfit
every day

WHAT THE STUDENTS
CONSIDERED THEIR
SCHOOL UNIFORMS.

Now arrange the circled letters to form
the surprise answer, as suggested by
the above cartoon.

## Print answer here

" ◯◯◯◯◯◯ - ◯ " ◯◯◯◯◯◯◯◯

# JUMBLE®

Unscramble these six Jumbles, one letter to each square, to form six ordinary words.

NABACA

REBARL

ENBILM

TROIGE

NASHEK

ACTOLE

I'll pay Big Tony $5,000 today and hold off on Tough Tom until next week

DIFFICULT FOR A BIG-TIME BETTOR TO DO.

Now arrange the circled letters to form the surprise answer, as suggested by the above cartoon.

**Print answer here**

◯◯◯◯◯◯◯ HIS ◯◯◯◯◯◯◯

167

# JUMBLE®

Unscramble these six Jumbles, one letter to each square, to form six ordinary words.

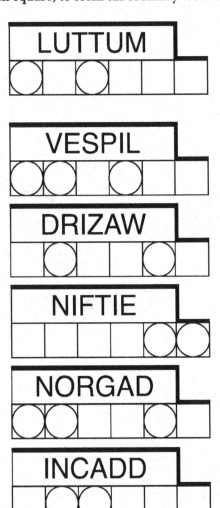

LUTTUM

VESPIL

DRIZAW

NIFTIE

NORGAD

INCADD

We'll let you know

...and if you buy right now, I'll ...

CARS

SALE

RESISTING THE FAST TALKER'S SALES PITCH WAS ---

Now arrange the circled letters to form the surprise answer, as suggested by the above cartoon.

**Print answer here**

◯◯◯◯ ◯◯◯◯◯ " ◯◯◯◯◯◯◯ "

# JUMBLE®

Unscramble these six Jumbles, one letter to
each square, to form six ordinary words.

DEDAHN

KEPPUE

MUCPIE

WEFURC

EGWAIH

CLOOSH

Oh!
That's so
gross

WHAT THE TIPSY
PARTYGOER DID WHEN
HE SWALLOWED THE
GOLDFISH WHOLE.

Now arrange the circled letters to form
the surprise answer, as suggested by
the above cartoon.

**Print answer here**

◯◯◯◯◯◯◯◯ THE ◯◯◯◯

# JUMBLE®

Unscramble these six Jumbles, one letter to each square, to form six ordinary words.

RUTIVE

LADUFE

TENCIE

FRYTAC

GURDED

MUGLEE

I've never had this much fun

THEIR DEEP SEA FISHING TRIP TURNED INTO A ---

Now arrange the circled letters to form the surprise answer, as suggested by the above cartoon.

**Print answer here**

" ◯◯◯◯◯ " ◯◯◯◯◯◯◯◯◯◯◯◯

# JUMBLE®

Unscramble these six Jumbles, one letter to each square, to form six ordinary words.

BAHFLE

PITTEO

TEBCOJ

ENOMAY

REEVER

VURSCY

You don't know talent!

Sorry, I can't use you

WHEN THE CONTORTIONIST FAILED THE AUDITION, HE WAS ---

Now arrange the circled letters to form the surprise answer, as suggested by the above cartoon.

*Print answer here* ⬡⬡⬡⬡ ⬡⬡⬡ OF ⬡⬡⬡⬡⬡

171

# JUMBLE®

Unscramble these six Jumbles, one letter to each square, to form six ordinary words.

LAPLOW

PYSEDE

YANTID

KUSTEM

CLEFEE

EDOSRL

First place is worth $5,000

WHAT THE PLAYERS RECEIVED WHEN THEY WON THE CURLING MATCH.

Now arrange the circled letters to form the surprise answer, as suggested by the above cartoon.

## Print answer here

" ◯◯◯◯◯ " ◯◯◯◯◯◯◯

# JUMBLE

Unscramble these six Jumbles, one letter to each square, to form six ordinary words.

YEMDOC

LUSTYS

DINIOE

THIFES

REBOFE

FRINEY

Let's go

What about the ice cream?

WHAT FIREMEN WILL DO WHEN THEY HEAR THE ALARM.

Now arrange the circled letters to form the surprise answer, as suggested by the above cartoon.

**Print answer here**

◯◯◯◯◯◯◯ THE ◯◯◯◯◯◯◯◯

# JUMBLE®

Unscramble these six Jumbles, one letter to each square, to form six ordinary words.

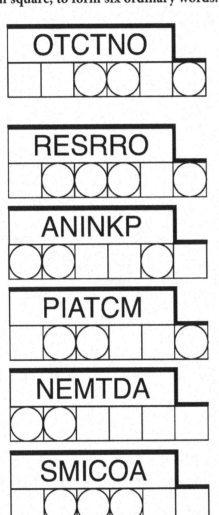

OTCTNO

RESRRO

ANINKP

PIATCM

NEMTDA

SMICOA

It's a good thing it's windy today or I'd be late for work.

It will still be easier than driving.

THE SAILBOAT PROVIDED THIS AFTER THE FERRY WAS SHUT DOWN.

Now arrange the circled letters to form the surprise answer, as suggested by the above cartoon.

**Print answer here**

" ⬡⬡⬡⬡ " ⬡⬡⬡⬡⬡⬡⬡⬡⬡⬡⬡⬡⬡⬡

# JUMBLE®

Unscramble these six Jumbles, one letter to each square, to form six ordinary words.

NHYEHP

ETANBE

ADRYFT

NICICL

YBSBAH

DILRAA

The way I said it was perfectly understandable. You need to listen better.

Can you repeat the last question? I didn't understand what you meant.

THE TEACHER THOUGHT THAT HER QUESTIONS FOR THE VERBAL U.S. GEOGRAPHY TEST WERE THIS.

Now arrange the circled letters to form the surprise answer, as suggested by the above cartoon.

**Print answer here**

# JUMBLE®

Unscramble these six Jumbles, one letter to each square, to form six ordinary words.

LOMSNA

LVTEEW

DEROAF

RBOHAC

UCIDTN

CIOYID

WITH SO MANY PEOPLE WANTING HER TO GAZE INTO HER CRYSTAL BALL, SHE DID THIS.

Now arrange the circled letters to form the surprise answer, as suggested by the above cartoon.

**Print answer here**

# JUMBLE®

Unscramble these six Jumbles, one letter to each square, to form six ordinary words.

TAOLWU

PAUCNK

GEEDPL

PEYTDU

SSLHAP

CTINEE

A few more seconds and I'll have this lock open.

IF THE SPY DIDN'T WANT TO GET CAUGHT BREAKING IN, SHE'D HAVE TO DO THIS.

Now arrange the circled letters to form the surprise answer, as suggested by the above cartoon.

**Print answer here**

# JUMBLE®

Unscramble these six Jumbles, one letter to each square, to form six ordinary words.

FARDOF

BUEERK

OEMISP

YMOEDB

MATICP

FNSLIU

He's perfect in this role.

It's just a costume!

I hate you!

EVEN THOUGH HE HAD MANY CO-STARS, IT WAS THIS THAT GOT HARRISON FORD RAVE REVIEWS IN "STAR WARS."

Now arrange the circled letters to form the surprise answer, as suggested by the above cartoon.

**Print answer here**

HIS ◯◯◯◯ ◯◯◯◯◯◯◯◯◯◯◯◯◯

# JUMBLE®

Unscramble these six Jumbles, one letter to
each square, to form six ordinary words.

NKRACY

DUKLER

OIONPS

TIEHRV

CAGINT

VSLIEW

Won't that
make it too
heavy?

We think
it's
going to
help.

WILBUR AND ORVILLE
MADE THIS WHEN THEY
CHOSE TO PUT TWO
WINGS ON THEIR PLANE.

Now arrange the circled letters to form
the surprise answer, as suggested by
the above cartoon.

*Print answer here*

THE "◯◯◯◯◯◯" ◯◯◯◯◯◯◯◯◯◯

# JUMBLE®

Unscramble these six Jumbles, one letter to
each square, to form six ordinary words.

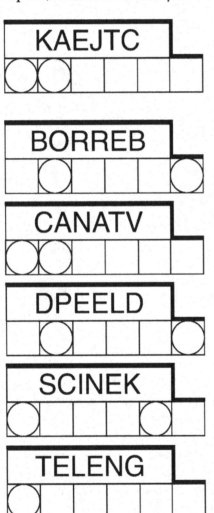

KAEJTC

BORREB

CANATV

DPEELD

SCINEK

TELENG

That's nothing. I won four Super Bowls and was MVP twice.

I won Super Bowl III, and I acted on television and in the movies.

THE CONVERSATION ABOUT
THEIR CAREERS SHOWED
THAT MONTANA AND
NAMATH WERE NOT ----

Now arrange the circled letters to form
the surprise answer, as suggested by
the above cartoon.

**Print answer here**

# JUMBLE®

Unscramble these six Jumbles, one letter to each square, to form six ordinary words.

PREETM

UCLANY

AHINEL

TERRAH

DOREWK

MENTAH

23 Red! 23 Red is the winner. Get ready to place your next bets.

I have 21. Everyone loses. Place your bets.

HANDLING THE BLACKJACK AND ROULETTE TABLES AT THE SAME TIME TURNED HIM INTO A ----

Now arrange the circled letters to form the surprise answer, as suggested by the above cartoon.

**Print answer here**

⬡⬡⬡⬡⬡⬡⬡ - ⬡⬡⬡⬡⬡⬡

# JUMBLE®

Unscramble these six Jumbles, one letter to
each square, to form six ordinary words.

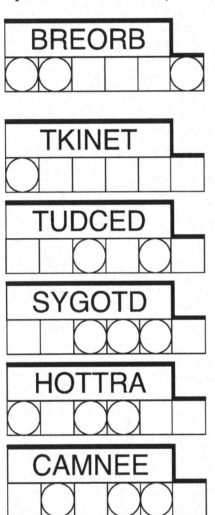

BREORB

TKINET

TUDCED

SYGOTD

HOTTRA

CAMNEE

Hélio has already won
here three times. I
wouldn't doubt if he
wins again today.

EVERYONE EXPECTED HIM
TO WIN THE RACE
BECAUSE HE HAD A ----

Now arrange the circled letters to form
the surprise answer, as suggested by
the above cartoon.

**Print answer here**

# JUMBLE®

Unscramble these six Jumbles, one letter to each square, to form six ordinary words.

APURRO

DASWHO

DACVIE

LEGNET

RATBEY

STARHH

WR-100 m butterfly 49.82 Michael Phelps

I don't need to break the record by much. Even a small margin would be good enough. I hope I trained hard enough. I shouldn't have eaten such a big breakfast this morning.

Hope you like silver, Michael.

WHAT HE HAD IN REGARD TO ATTEMPTING TO BREAK THE WORLD RECORD.

Now arrange the circled letters to form the surprise answer, as suggested by the above cartoon.

### Print answer here

# Answers

1. **Jumbles:** LANKY BIPED POUNCE BEWAIL
   **Answer:** What the sleeping recruits felt like when they heard the bugle — BLOWN "UP"

2. **Jumbles:** FRAME GLEAM LEVITY POCKET
   **Answer:** When they viewed the full moon from the mountain top, they couldn't — GET OVER IT

3. **Jumbles:** FUSSY CRUSH KISMET JACKET
   **Answer:** Why the boxer joined the soccer team — JUST FOR "KICKS"

4. **Jumbles:** BLOAT EAGLE THRIVE UNLOCK
   **Answer:** When the dentist and his manicurist wife fought, it was — TOOTH AND NAIL

5. **Jumbles:** BAKED USURP CUDDLE CANDID
   **Answer:** Where ideals can come from — LADIES

6. **Jumbles:** CHICK QUOTA ECZEMA BECOME
   **Answer:** What the boomerang champion sought when he lost the contest — A "COMEBACK"

7. **Jumbles:** TEMPO UNWED RADISH FACADE
   **Answer:** The students admired the archaeologist because he was — DOWN TO EARTH

8. **Jumbles:** BOGUS CLEFT HELIUM PHYSIC
   **Answer:** What it takes to spot a distant ice site — EYE SIGHT

9. **Jumbles:** WEARY EPOCH OUTFIT RAREFY
   **Answer:** When the charter pilot's son took over the business, it became an — HEIR FORCE

10. **Jumbles:** FUDGE MURKY WINNOW JERSEY
    **Answer:** The first thing the teen took when he got his driver's license — A "JOY" RIDE

11. **Jumbles:** NIPPY LOOSE BEYOND DEFACE
    **Answer:** What air travelers get, even in first class — "PLANE" FOOD

12. **Jumbles:** BUILT ALTAR HUNTER OVERDO
    **Answer:** When the wheel was invented, it created a — REVOLUTION

13. **Jumbles:** JETTY MOUSE GAMBOL TYPHUS
    **Answer:** In a bar, sitting down can result in — BOTTOMS UP

14. **Jumbles:** IDIOM AUDIT GRASSY TETHER
    **Answer:** When the city slicker tried milking a cow, the result was — AN "UDDER" MESS

15. **Jumbles:** LIBEL PIKER UNCURL HANDLE
    **Answer:** One result of being riled — IDLER

16. **Jumbles:** DRAWL GRAIN POORLY WORTHY
    **Answer:** A tickets mix-up can result in a — ROW ROW

17. **Jumbles:** RAJAH BRIBE EFFACE INDIGO
    **Answer:** A busy blacksmith will do this — "FORGE" AHEAD

18. **Jumbles:** SKUNK FEWER MUFFIN TURTLE
    **Answer:** He was named taxidermist of the year because he — KNEW HIS "STUFF"

19. **Jumbles:** FEINT AMITY WIZARD SMILES
    **Answer:** A middle-age paunch can be a — "WAIST" OF TIME

20. **Jumbles:** NOISY AHEAD UPTOWN BAZAAR
    **Answer:** What a cookbook author will do — EAT HIS WORDS

21. **Jumbles:** PEONY FAMED BRIDLE EASILY
    **Answer:** Why the young ball player didn't have a steady girlfriend — HE PLAYED THE "FIELD"

22. **Jumbles:** ICILY BRAND BUTANE MUFFLE
    **Answer:** What it takes to ship a package cross country — A "BUNDLE"

23. **Jumbles:** DICED LIGHT FACIAL GIBLET
    **Answer:** Giving Junior a heap of educational toys made him a — "GIFTED" CHILD

24. **Jumbles:** MAIZE CHANT ADROIT FINITE
    **Answer:** What he paid when he hired the tax advisor — ATTENTION

25. **Jumbles:** ABASH DRAMA SNITCH ABSORB
    **Answer:** The secretary concentrated on this — THE SHORT HAND

26. **Jumbles:** MOUNT ANISE HANSOM SMUDGE
    **Answer:** What the male model received when he posed in the suit — A "HANDSOME" SUM

27. **Jumbles:** VITAL IVORY NIBBLE SLOGAN
    **Answer:** Watching an ironworker high on a skyscraper can be — "RIVETING"

28. **Jumbles:** BURLY MOLDY PARLOR ADRIFT
    **Answer:** What he turned into when he went to skydiving school — A DROP OUT

29. **Jumbles:** EXUDE LIMIT CHARGE UNEASY
    **Answer:** When the mechanic installed the new muffler, it was — "EXHAUSTING"

30. **Jumbles:** CUBIT CRANK GROUCH FORAGE
    **Answer:** What he drove when he bought a used car — A TOUGH BARGAIN

31. **Jumbles:** IGLOO KNEEL UPWARD FLUNKY
    **Answer:** When she changed her hair color, it was — TO "DYE" FOR

32. **Jumbles:** MOUSY DOWNY MUSLIN PENMAN
    **Answer:** What it cost the London mogul to lose some pounds — SOME POUNDS

33. **Jumbles:** TRULY SOUSE IMMUNE HEALTH
    **Answer:** What the businessmen read before breakfast — THE MENU

34. **Jumbles:** BATCH PRONE CHERUB MEASLY
    **Answer:** What the teen-agers turned into after a dip in the ocean — BEACH COMBERS

35. **Jumbles:** DUNCE OZONE FRIEZE BLUISH
    **Answer:** When the cats performed for the animal trainer, he was — "LIONIZED"

36. **Jumbles:** VAGUE TYPED URCHIN MARVEL
    **Answer:** What the surgeon turned into at the annual party — A REAL CUT UP

37. **Jumbles:** SAVOR SWISH GLANCE MAMMAL
    **Answer:** When the artist was asked what was behind the painting, he said it — WAS A CANVAS

38. **Jumbles:** MUSIC CHAFF COHORT MAYHEM
    **Answer:** How one can get aches — FROM CHASE

39. **Jumbles:** NOTCH ADULT GOITER SAVORY
    **Answer:** When the ballet star helped her dancemate, she did a — GOOD "TURN"

40. **Jumbles:** LEAFY THINK HITHER PASTRY
    **Answer:** What happened when he got the bill for the roof? — HE HIT THE "RAFTERS"

41. **Jumbles:** GRAVE OBESE CRABBY SUBMIT
    **Answer:** When vandals used spray paint on the steps, police said it was — A STAIR "CASE"

42. **Jumbles:** MINER BAGGY GUITAR UPHELD
    **Answer:** What the couple got in the lighting store — A "BRIGHT" IDEA

43. **Jumbles:** TWILL PARCH SECEDE ZEALOT
    **Answer:** Why the young king refused to wear a crown — IT WAS OLD "HAT"

44. **Jumbles:** MINCE ALIAS NIMBLE SHANTY
    **Answer:** The workers described the nasty tycoon as — A MAN OF "MEANS"

45. **Jumbles:** ABIDE SYNOD ABDUCT GUNNER
**Answer:** When Mom sewed the hole in his sock, she considered it a — "DARN" NUISANCE

46. **Jumbles:** BASIN CHESS MARLIN HIATUS
**Answer:** One might say that the movie stars turned the demolition derby into a — "SMASH" HIT

47. **Jumbles:** GAWKY CLUCK THROAT TRUANT
**Answer:** When the phony trapeze artist fell into the net, he was — CAUGHT IN THE "ACT"

48. **Jumbles:** SILKY FUROR OCCULT PARADE
**Answer:** What a boxer will fight for that a woman has — A PURSE

49. **Jumbles:** GULCH PANIC SPRUCE BICEPS
**Answer:** When the crew lined up for haircuts, the submarine became — A "CLIPPER" SHIP

50. **Jumbles:** COUPE ELDER LARYNX DELUXE
**Answer:** What the janitor did when he played poker — HE "CLEANED" UP

51. **Jumbles:** UNCAP GLORY CHISEL BOTTLE
**Answer:** What the tallest player did when the team stayed in a hotel — SLEPT "LONGER"

52. **Jumbles:** ELEGY DECAY ORPHAN LOCATE
**Answer:** Some homemakers preserve summer vegetables because — THEY "CAN"

53. **Jumbles:** TRUTH PLAIT FUSION GRISLY
**Answer:** What happened when his grip was lost — HE LOST HIS "GRIP"

54. **Jumbles:** CIVIL CREEL GOATEE ALPACA
**Answer:** When the skinny little convict gained weight in prison, he was — AT "LARGE"

55. **Jumbles:** IRONY WEIGH WHINNY SUNDAE
**Answer:** She was attracted to the card shark because he had — "WINNING" WAYS

56. **Jumbles:** PERKY LATHE RADIAL PESTLE
**Answer:** In the old west, a six-shooter was an — EARLY "SETTLER"

57. **Jumbles:** LEAVE POKED FETISH MARTYR
**Answer:** She dumped her boyfriend because she wanted a future and he — HAD A PAST

58. **Jumbles:** MEALY RABBI DOUBLE CIPHER
**Answer:** What the warden did when the crooked barber escaped — "COMBED" THE AREA

59. **Jumbles:** PRIOR FINIS INFANT MINGLE
**Answer:** Why the balloons went up — "INFLATION"

60. **Jumbles:** NUDGE BILGE FLORID DREDGE
**Answer:** What the violinist enjoyed doing in the garden — "FIDDLING"

61. **Jumbles:** LISLE ADMIT CLOTHE KNIGHT
**Answer:** Being loose with money can lead to this — "TIGHT" TIMES

62. **Jumbles:** FLANK ENJOY MOTION FALTER
**Answer:** When the celebrity was seated in the back row, he — TOOK AFFRONT

63. **Jumbles:** ENSUE FLAKE ADJOIN VERIFY
**Answer:** The referee thought the defensive lineman was — OFFENSIVE

64. **Jumbles:** UTTER SQUAB TRUISM INDUCE
**Answer:** When the cook drained the huge pot of pasta, it was — QUITE A "STRAIN"

65. **Jumbles:** GROOM DRYLY COUPON INVENT
**Answer:** Easy to become when modeling fur coats — A "COVER" GIRL

66. **Jumbles:** MOUND BLESS FOSSIL WHEEZE
**Answer:** When the doughnut maker bought out his partner, he got the — "HOLE" BUSINESS

67. **Jumbles:** QUILT METAL GIGOLO INNING
**Answer:** How the electrician described the preacher's sermon — "ILLUMINATING"

68. **Jumbles:** VERVE BRIAR INVERT DURESS
**Answer:** When the aspiring poet got an idea during the night, he went from — BED TO VERSE

69. **Jumbles:** VOCAL GRIMY LICHEN SHOULD
**Answer:** The cheerleader said her beau, the sprinter, was — "DASHING"

70. **Jumbles:** GROUP BISON LAYOFF NATURE
**Answer:** When they went to the shark movie, it was — ABOUT A "FIN"

71. **Jumbles:** BOOTY HAVEN OUTLAW OXYGEN
**Answer:** Where he went when he stopped drinking — ON THE WAGON

72. **Jumbles:** TARDY BLAZE HARROW MALADY
**Answer:** When the seer read their fortune, she — HAD A "BALL"

73. **Jumbles:** NIECE VALVE IMPEDE SLEIGH
**Answer:** The escapee broke into the tannery because it was a — "HIDING" PLACE

74. **Jumbles:** DECRY UNCLE MALTED NUMBER
**Answer:** A beauty queen will make her entrance to — ENTRANCE

75. **Jumbles:** SIXTY LOONY THEORY SHAKEN
**Answer:** What the boxer did when his girlfriend's little brother appeared — TOOK IT ON THE SHIN

76. **Jumbles:** ASSAY GUEST DEADLY ARCTIC
**Answer:** When the rain ruined her hairdo, she was — "DIS-TRESSED"

77. **Jumbles:** TWICE FLOOD WALLOP CANYON
**Answer:** What the tenant got when he rented the basement apartment — THE "LOW-DOWN"

78. **Jumbles:** RUSTY POWER BIGAMY COMPEL
**Answer:** When the runabout stalled, it turned into — A "WOE" BOAT

79. **Jumbles:** SNACK ABYSS OUTCRY VIABLE
**Answer:** A good way to improve the view at a football game — BINOCULARS

80. **Jumbles:** BLANK JOINT GRUBBY COUGAR
**Answer:** Filling the gas tank these days can leave you — "BURNING"

81. **Jumbles:** OWING GUILD POPLIN KIMONO
**Answer:** The blue-eyed blonde led the bird watchers because she was — GOOD "LOOKING"

82. **Jumbles:** POISE QUEUE BYWORD VARIED
**Answer:** This can ruin a relationship — "BRIDE" IDEAS

83. **Jumbles:** CHOKE LUNGE THORAX BUNION
**Answer:** When the magician made his beautiful helper disappear, she was — NOTHING TO LOOK AT

84. **Jumbles:** AZURE SHYLY FURROW FAUCET
**Answer:** When the manager kept changing pitchers, the southpaw — WAS "LEFT"

85. **Jumbles:** GAVEL TULIP CIRCUS MAGPIE
**Answer:** "Pirates" can give you this — SEA TRIP

86. **Jumbles:** SKULK CROUP MODISH NOUGAT
**Answer:** What the cat show winner turned into — A GLAMOUR "PUSS"

87. **Jumbles:** BATON FORGO HUMBLE COWARD
**Answer:** When the icicle fell on the mailman's head, he was — OUT "COLD"

88. **Jumbles:** FELON CREEK PREFER AVENUE
**Answer:** What the feuding neighbors had on the Fourth of July — A "FLARE" UP

89. **Jumbles:** FAVOR CEASE JARGON DRIVEL
**Answer:** The waiter won the tennis match because he was a — GOOD "SERVER"

90. **Jumbles:** ENACT FLUTE EMBODY WHOLLY
**Answer:** When the old-time telegraph operator sent his hourly message, it was — ON THE "DOT"

91. **Jumbles:** LYRIC PIETY FLORAL PEPSIN
**Answer:** The actor used greasepaint because he had a —
"SLIPPERY" ROLE

92. **Jumbles:** FATAL JADED NICELY CAVORT
**Answer:** When her fiance got hot under the collar, she ended
up with — COLD FEET

93. **Jumbles:** POACH TASTY SADIST MISHAP
**Answer:** The convict enjoyed sitting in the sun because he
had a — "SHADY" PAST

94. **Jumbles:** ROBOT QUEST ZITHER CATNIP
**Answer:** When the ex-strikeout king sold cars, he used his —
BEST "PITCH"

95. **Jumbles:** EXERT VOUCH WEEVIL NEWEST
**Answer:** What the bath shop did when business soured —
THREW IN THE TOWEL

96. **Jumbles:** VIXEN AGONY MODIFY BEFALL
**Answer:** For a traffic court judge, it's always a — "FINE" DAY

97. **Jumbles:** BEFOG DOUBT CRAYON BYGONE
**Answer:** What he bid at the auction — GOOD BYE

98. **Jumbles:** TAKEN PLUME COLUMN INDUCT
**Answer:** The carpenter fired his helper because he —
COULDN'T "CUT" IT

99. **Jumbles:** STUNG WHISK AUTUMN IMPORT
**Answer:** When the cleaner ruined the lawyer's outfit, he
faced a — SUIT SUIT

100. **Jumbles:** ABOVE TOOTH PLURAL TARTAR
**Answer:** Easy to get without a lot of trouble —
A LOT OF TROUBLE

101. **Jumbles:** CASTE QUAKE STICKY CENSUS
**Answer:** When the concert pianist performed, he exhibited
his — "KEYS" TO SUCCESS

102. **Jumbles:** SOAPY PLUSH PUDDLE BLAZER
**Answer:** Acceptable when renting a beach umbrella —
A "SHADY" DEAL

103. **Jumbles:** PYLON GIVEN INFLUX DISOWN
**Answer:** Done by a laborer when he gets the job —
FILLS THE "OPENING"

104. **Jumbles:** PRIME CRAFT SEPTIC OUTWIT
**Answer:** She married a novelist because he was —
MISTER "WRITE"

105. **Jumbles:** COUGH COLIC TAWDRY LAVISH
**Answer:** What the tycoon resorted to when his assets were
frozen — COLD CASH

106. **Jumbles:** MADAM GAUGE KERNEL RUBBER
**Answer:** Although she was stuck-up, her looks made him —
"UNGLUED"

107. **Jumbles:** TULLE SCARF POROUS HANGAR
**Answer:** What she got when the sugar daddy gave her his
credit card — A "CHARGE" OUT OF IT

108. **Jumbles:** CROON TACKY FARINA BRUTAL
**Answer:** This takes some study before a big purchase —
A BANK ACCOUNT

109. **Jumbles:** FRAUD BUMPY PUSHER JAUNTY
**Answer:** What a single girl shouldn't look for when she's
looking for this — A HUSBAND

110. **Jumbles:** MAUVE DEMON ENTICE AWEIGH
**Answer:** When the banker shed his suit for sweats, he felt like
a — "CHANGED" MAN

111. **Jumbles:** HEFTY KAPOK JURIST EMPLOY
**Answer:** What a mouthful of gossip can result in —
AN EARFUL

112. **Jumbles:** GROIN EVENT DENTAL HERALD
**Answer:** When the doctor didn't charge him, the young
patient was — "TREATED"

113. **Jumbles:** DUMPY OPIUM HALLOW DONKEY
**Answer:** What the schoolboys did when they met the
basketball star — LOOKED "UP" TO HIM

114. **Jumbles:** KNELL ACRID WALNUT ALKALI
**Answer:** How the baker won the town election —
IN A CAKEWALK

115. **Jumbles:** PECAN CATCH HAIRDO PREFIX
**Answer:** What the groom did when he married the math
teacher — CARRIED THE "ONE"

116. **Jumbles:** FAITH VAPOR EXODUS HANDED
**Answer:** The owner didn't repair the roof because it was —
OVER HIS HEAD

117. **Jumbles:** SHAKY AROMA TOUCHY LEGUME
**Answer:** The kind of dress worn by a ghost — SEE-THROUGH

118. **Jumbles:** WHOSE BOUGH SCROLL DAMASK
**Answer:** What he used when he was fishing for a good
novel — A BOOKWORM

119. **Jumbles:** GOURD ALBUM SWERVE HOPPER
**Answer:** When he rolled a perfect game, he was —
"BOWLED" OVER

120. **Jumbles:** FRIAR AIDED MIDWAY FOIBLE
**Answer:** How he described his parrot — A WORDY BIRDIE

121. **Jumbles:** WALTZ DUCHY GAINED MISERY
**Answer:** Where you can find the most fish — IN THE MIDDLE

122. **Jumbles:** LIMBO WHEEL STUPID BEHOLD
**Answer:** When their new house was completed, the couple
was — BUILD BILLED

123. **Jumbles:** PUTTY SNARL BEACON BASKET
**Answer:** What the broker gave the nervous investor —
A "STOCK" REPLY

124. **Jumbles:** AWASH HEAVY DOMINO GRAVEN
**Answer:** A deposit at the blood bank is a —
GOOD WAY TO "SAVE"

125. **Jumbles:** BALKY PRIZE AUBURN THRASH
**Answer:** What the garbage man said when the customer
complained — "RUBBISH"

126. **Jumbles:** TEPID SPURN CANNED ENOUGH
**Answer:** What the dietitian did when the English patient lost
weight — GAINED "POUNDS"

127. **Jumbles:** PIANO GUILT CANINE MYSELF
**Answer:** This can make for a "genial" evening — GIN AND ALE

128. **Jumbles:** QUEER INEPT BREACH SYSTEM
**Answer:** What the executives needed when they met for a
bite — TEETH

129. **Jumbles:** ABHOR IMBUE SAILOR INJECT
**Answer:** The groomer brushed the show horse's hair because
it was — HIS "MANE" JOB

130. **Jumbles:** LINEN HONOR SICKEN TEAPOT
**Answer:** Needed when buying and playing a vintage
violin — "C" NOTES

131. **Jumbles:** DAUNT LEECH BELLOW FEDORA
**Answer:** Too many square meals can make one —
WELL "ROUNDED"

132. **Jumbles:** PRINT KNAVE GRATIS AGHAST
**Answer:** What the couple went through buying the right
house — THEIR SAVINGS

133. **Jumbles:** MERGE NUTTY EGOISM JETSAM
**Answer:** How the couple described the Grand Canyon —
JUST "GORGES"

134. **Jumbles:** AFIRE DITTY USEFUL PIRATE
**Answer:** What the scout experienced when he hiked through
the woods — A FIELD "TRIP"

135. **Jumbles:** OPERA BANJO TRIBAL SUBWAY
**Answer:** When the players began fighting, the game turned
into — BASE BRAWL

136. **Jumbles:** NOOSE SHEEP DITHER VIRTUE
**Answer:** What the sarge said to the sleeping recruit —
RISE AND SHINE

137. **Jumbles:** JUMPY CHUTE PURVEY JANGLE
**Answer:** No matter what is served, this will make it
attractive — HUNGER

138. **Jumbles:** TEASE CURRY SPORTY ABUSED
**Answer:** The mattress was guaranteed so the couple could — "REST" ASSURED

139. **Jumbles:** PILOT GORGE BUMPER DISCUS
**Answer:** When the tattoo artist put a butterfly on her leg, she was — "IMPRESSED"

140. **Jumbles:** COACH FEVER CORPSE TRIPLE
**Answer:** What the sheriff always has in a western movie — A "STAR" ROLE

141. **Jumbles:** BELLE MAXIM PLACID VANITY
**Answer:** Even a king takes a back seat to this in a poker game — AN ACE

142. **Jumbles:** AWARD BANAL SUCKLE ADDUCE
**Answer:** When he tried his hand at archery, he discovered it had — "DRAWBACKS"

143. **Jumbles:** PAGAN TOXIC BISECT FROTHY
**Answer:** How a night out on the town left him — IN A "TIGHT" SPOT

144. **Jumbles:** POPPY SWOOP ROTATE TINGLE
**Answer:** What a photographer can do with a bored model — GET "SNAPPY"

145. **Jumbles:** PEACE LATCH MISFIT HELPER
**Answer:** In for dinner, but frequently out all night — FALSE TEETH

146. **Jumbles:** NOISE PANSY SYMBOL KETTLE
**Answer:** What it takes to become a ballroom dancer — LOTS OF "STEPS"

147. **Jumbles:** MANLY LEGAL ELIXIR ICEBOX
**Answer:** When the manager let off steam, he was — "BOILING"

148. **Jumbles:** BANDY ELITE FEMALE ACTUAL
**Answer:** It doesn't exist at the equator — LATITUDE

149. **Jumbles:** EMBER DAILY ENJOIN BURIAL
**Answer:** When he crossed the cops, the stool pigeon became a — JAILBIRD

150. **Jumbles:** HASTY AFTER KOSHER TYPING
**Answer:** What the hairdresser did for the long-haired brunette — "SET" HER RIGHT

151. **Jumbles:** HUMAN WEDGE DENOTE HEREBY
**Answer:** The farmer's simple philosophy was — DOWN TO "EARTH"

152. **Jumbles:** KNOWN LITHE LIQUOR TROUGH
**Answer:** What the electrician did while he recovered from his injury — "LIGHT" WORK

153. **Jumbles:** YACHT IDIOT FLABBY PERMIT
**Answer:** When they met on horseback, she was on the — "BRIDAL" PATH

154. **Jumbles:** UNITY BASSO CELERY TIMELY
**Answer:** The mailman received an advanced degree because he was a — MAN OF "LETTERS"

155. **Jumbles:** RAPID EMPTY INLAID COUPLE
**Answer:** What she experienced when she danced in her new shoes — PAIN AT THE "PUMP"

156. **Jumbles:** POUND PLAID HAUNCH WOEFUL
**Answer:** The police roadblock led to a — HOLDUP HOLDUP

157. **Jumbles:** JULEP CAMEO PURPLE DEBTOR
**Answer:** What the farmer saw when he visited the junkyard — A "BUMPER" CROP

158. **Jumbles:** EVOKE FAULT SINFUL GOLFER
**Answer:** She chased the real estate developer because he had — "LOTS" TO OFFER

159. **Jumbles:** ANKLE HITCH BAKERY KITTEN
**Answer:** What she thought when their paths crossed on the trail — TAKE A HIKE

160. **Jumbles:** LINGO ARDOR MARTIN KENNEL
**Answer:** Wise to do when it's "love at first sight" — LOOK AGAIN.

161. **Jumbles:** CALMLY HOMING COBALT FESTAL ISLAND HAMLET
**Answer:** What it took to get his son through college ALMOST ALL HE HAD

162. **Jumbles:** POPLAR MEDLEY BUREAU MEMBER BEHEAD JAGGED
**Answer:** The crooked baker was arrested for — HOMEMADE "BREAD"

163. **Jumbles:** CLERGY MALLET BOLERO DURESS BLEACH MASCOT
**Answer:** What the students considered their school uniforms — "CLASS-Y" CLOTHES

164. **Jumbles:** CABANA BARREL NIMBLE GOITER SHAKEN LOCATE
**Answer:** Difficult for a big-time bettor to do — BALANCE HIS BOOKIES

165. **Jumbles:** TUMULT PELVIS WIZARD FINITE DRAGON CANDID
**Answer:** Resisting the fast talker's sales pitch was — MIND OVER "PATTER"

166. **Jumbles:** HANDED UPKEEP PUMICE CURFEW AWEIGH SCHOOL
**Answer:** What the tipsy partygoer did when he swallowed the goldfish whole — ESCHEWED THE CHEW

167. **Jumbles:** VIRTUE FEUDAL ENTICE CRAFTY DRUDGE LEGUME
**Answer:** Their deep sea fishing trip turned into a — "REEL" ADVENTURE

168. **Jumbles:** BEHALF TIPTOE OBJECT YEOMAN REVERE SCURVY
**Answer:** When the contortionist failed the audition, he was — BENT OUT OF SHAPE

169. **Jumbles:** WALLOP SPEEDY DAINTY MUSKET FLEECE SOLDER
**Answer:** What the players received when they won the curling match — "SWEEP" STAKES

170. **Jumbles:** COMEDY STYLUS IODINE FETISH BEFORE FINERY
**Answer:** What firemen will do when they hear the alarm — DESERT THE DESSERT

171. **Jumbles:** COTTON ERRORS NAPKIN IMPACT TANDEM MOSAIC
**Answer:** This sailboat provided this after the ferry was shut down — "MAST" TRANSPORTATION

172. **Jumbles:** HYPHEN BEATEN DRAFTY CLINIC SHABBY RADIAL
**Answer:** The teacher thought that her questions for the verbal U.S. geography test were this — CLEARLY STATED

173. **Jumbles:** SALMON TWELVE FEDORA BROACH INDUCT IDIOCY
**Answer:** With so many people wanting her to gaze into her crystal ball, she did this — MADE A FORTUNE

174. **Jumbles:** OUTLAW UNPACK PLEDGE DEPUTY SPLASH ENTICE
**Answer:** If the spy didn't want to get caught breaking in, she'd have to do this — PICK UP THE PACE

175. **Jumbles:** AFFORD REBUKE IMPOSE EMBODY IMPACT SINFUL
**Answer:** Even though he had many co-stars, it was this that got Harrison Ford rave reviews in "Star Wars" — HIS SOLO PERFORMANCE

176. **Jumbles:** CRANKY LURKED POISON THRIVE ACTING SWIVEL
**Answer:** Wilbur and Orville made this when they chose to put two wings on their plane — THE "WRIGHT" DECISION

177. **Jumbles:** JACKET ROBBER VACANT PEDDLE SICKEN GENTLE
**Answer:** The conversation about their careers showed that Montana and Namath were not — AVERAGE JOES

178. **Jumbles:** TEMPER LUNACY INHALE RATHER WORKED ANTHEM
**Answer:** Handling the blackjack and roulette tables at the same time turned him into a — WHEELER-DEALER

179. **Jumbles:** ROBBER KITTEN DEDUCT STODGY THROAT MENACE
**Answer:** Everyone expected him to win the race because he had a — GOOD TRACK RECORD

180. **Jumbles:** UPROAR SHADOW ADVICE GENTLE BETRAY THRASH
**Answer:** What he had in regard to attempting to break the world record — SECOND THOUGHTS

# Need More Jumbles?

Order any of these books through your bookseller or call Triumph Books toll-free at 800-888-4741.

## Jumble® Books

### More than 175 puzzles each!

**Cowboy Jumble®**
• ISBN: 978-1-62937-355-3

**Jammin' Jumble®**
• ISBN: 978-1-57243-844-6

**Java Jumble®**
• ISBN: 978-1-60078-415-6

**Jet Set Jumble®**
• ISBN: 978-1-60078-353-1

**Jolly Jumble®**
• ISBN: 978-1-60078-214-5

**Jumble® Anniversary**
• ISBN: 987-1-62937-734-6

**Jumble® Ballet**
• ISBN: 978-1-62937-616-5

**Jumble® Birthday**
• ISBN: 978-1-62937-652-3

**Jumble® Celebration**
• ISBN: 978-1-60078-134-6

**Jumble® Champion**
• ISBN: 978-1-62937-870-1

**Jumble® Coronation**
• ISBN: 978-1-62937-976-0

**Jumble® Cuisine**
• ISBN: 978-1-62937-735-3

**Jumble® Drag Race**
• ISBN: 978-1-62937-483-3

**Jumble® Ever After**
• ISBN: 978-1-62937-785-8

**Jumble® Explorer**
• ISBN: 978-1-60078-854-3

**Jumble® Explosion**
• ISBN: 978-1-60078-078-3

**Jumble® Fever**
• ISBN: 978-1-57243-593-3

**Jumble® Galaxy**
• ISBN: 978-1-60078-583-2

**Jumble® Garden**
• ISBN: 978-1-62937-653-0

**Jumble® Genius**
• ISBN: 978-1-57243-896-5

**Jumble® Geography**
• ISBN: 978-1-62937-615-8

**Jumble® Getaway**
• ISBN: 978-1-60078-547-4

**Jumble® Gold**
• ISBN: 978-1-62937-354-6

**Jumble® Health**
• ISBN: 978-1-63727-085-1

**Jumble® Jackpot**
• ISBN: 978-1-57243-897-2

**Jumble® Jailbreak**
• ISBN: 978-1-62937-002-6

**Jumble® Jambalaya**
• ISBN: 978-1-60078-294-7

**Jumble® Jitterbug**
• ISBN: 978-1-60078-584-9

**Jumble® Journey**
• ISBN: 978-1-62937-549-6

**Jumble® Jubilation**
• ISBN: 978-1-62937-784-1

**Jumble® Jubilee**
• ISBN: 978-1-57243-231-4

**Jumble® Juggernaut**
• ISBN: 978-1-60078-026-4

**Jumble® Kingdom**
• ISBN: 978-1-62937-079-8

**Jumble® Knockout**
• ISBN: 978-1-62937-078-1

**Jumble® Madness**
• ISBN: 978-1-892049-24-7

**Jumble® Magic**
• ISBN: 978-1-60078-795-9

**Jumble® Mania**
• ISBN: 978-1-57243-697-8

**Jumble® Marathon**
• ISBN: 978-1-60078-944-1

**Jumble® Masterpiece**
• ISBN: 978-1-62937-916-6

**Jumble® Neighbor**
• ISBN: 978-1-62937-845-9

**Jumble® Parachute**
• ISBN: 978-1-62937-548-9

**Jumble® Party**
• ISBN: 978-1-63727-008-0

**Jumble® Safari**
• ISBN: 978-1-60078-675-4

**Jumble® Sensation**
• ISBN: 978-1-60078-548-1

**Jumble® Skyscraper**
• ISBN: 978-1-62937-869-5

**Jumble® Symphony**
• ISBN: 978-1-62937-131-3

**Jumble® Theater**
• ISBN: 978-1-62937-484-0

**Jumble® Time Machine: 1972**
• ISBN: 978-1-63727-082-0

**Jumble® Trouble**
• ISBN: 978-1-62937-917-3

**Jumble® University**
• ISBN: 978-1-62937-001-9

**Jumble® Unleashed**
• ISBN: 978-1-62937-844-2

**Jumble® Vacation**
• ISBN: 978-1-60078-796-6

**Jumble® Wedding**
• ISBN: 978-1-62937-307-2

**Jumble® Workout**
• ISBN: 978-1-60078-943-4

**Jump, Jive and Jumble®**
• ISBN: 978-1-60078-215-2

**Lunar Jumble®**
• ISBN: 978-1-60078-853-6

**Monster Jumble®**
• ISBN: 978-1-62937-213-6

**Mystic Jumble®**
• ISBN: 978-1-62937-130-6

**Rainy Day Jumble®**
• ISBN: 978-1-60078-352-4

**Royal Jumble®**
• ISBN: 978-1-60078-738-6

**Sports Jumble®**
• ISBN: 978-1-57243-113-3

**Summer Fun Jumble®**
• ISBN: 978-1-57243-114-0

**Touchdown Jumble®**
• ISBN: 978-1-62937-212-9

## Oversize Jumble® Books

### More than 500 puzzles!

**Colossal Jumble®**
• ISBN: 978-1-57243-490-5

**Jumbo Jumble®**
• ISBN: 978-1-57243-314-4

## Jumble® Crosswords™

### More than 175 puzzles!

**Jumble® Crosswords™**
• ISBN: 978-1-57243-347-2